RAYMOND CHANDLER in HOLLYWOOD

RAYMOND CHANDLER
IN HOLLYWOOD

by
AL CLARK

SILMAN-JAMES PRESS   LOS ANGELES

First Edition
10 9 8 7 6 5 4 3 2 1

Library of Congress Cataloging-in-Publication Data

Clark, Al.
Raymond Chandler in Hollywood / by Al Clark
p. cm.
Originally published: London; New York : Proteus. 1982
1. Chandler, Raymond, 1888-1959—Film and video adaptations.
2. Chandler, Raymond. 1888-1959—Motion picture plays.
3. Detective and mystery films—History and criticism.
4. American fiction—Film and video adaptations.
5. Marlowe, Philip (Fictitious character)
6. Hollywood (Los Angeles, Calif.)
I. Title.
PS3505.H3224Z6   1996   813'.52--dc20   96-7955
ISBN: 1-879505-29-0

Cover design and illustration by Wade Lageose, Art Hotel

Printed and bound in the United States of America

Silman-James Press
1181 Angelo Drive
Beverly Hills, CA 90210

*In memory of David and Marion Clark
and for Jason, Louise, and Lesley*

CONTENTS

ACKNOWLEDGMENTS

When I began to research this book for its original publication in 1982, the intention was simple enough: to chronicle Raymond Chandler's years in Hollywood, either as the provider of source material—his six filmed novels have so far yielded ten movies—or as a screenwriter, an activity to which he applied himself with increasing weariness and contempt between 1943 and 1950.

The practice, inevitably, was a little more complicated. Arriving in California with only a hotel reservation, a list of names, and a sense of urgency, I began a process that took on an increasingly surreal resemblance to detective work. By the end of the first day, I had discovered that five directors and four writers whom I wanted to interview were already dead, and that one actress was an invalid and I could only speak to her nurse. What started as a labor of curiosity became a race against mortality.

Given these circumstances, I was particularly grateful to the survivors of these films who shared their recollections with me. Some remembered a great deal; others hardly anything. Several could only speak to me on the telephone; a few entertained me with a generosity beyond mere civility. I would like to thank Lewis Allen, Lauren Bacall, Paul Bogart, Philip Carey, Candy Clark, Edward Dmytryk, Steve Fisher, Melvin Frank, David Zelag Goodman, Dorothy Hannah, Alfred Hitchcock, John Houseman, Fred MacMurray, George Montgomery, Robert Montgomery, Czenzi Ormonde, John Paxton, Dilys Powell, Dick Richards, Stirling Silliphant, Barry Sullivan, Audrey Totter, and, particularly, Nina van Pallandt. Two of them had already died by the time the book was first published; several more have since followed.

These books were useful in different ways. Some are quoted, others were simply of factual assistance: *The Life of Raymond Chandler*, Frank MacShane. *Raymond Chandler Speaking*, ed. Dorothy Gardiner and Kathrine Sorley Walker. *The World of Raymond Chandler*, ed. Miriam Gross. *The Day of the Locust*, Nathanael West. *Los Angeles*, Reyner Banham. *Play It As It Lays*, Joan Didion. *The Detective in Film*, William K. Everson. *The Detective in Hollywood*, Jon Tuska. *The Pat Hobby Stories*, F. Scott Fitzgerald. *Double Indemnity*, James M. Cain. *Billy Wilder in Hollywood*, Maurice Zolotow. *Hollywood in the Forties*, Charles Higham and Joel Greenberg. *Front and Centre*, John Houseman. *Raymond Chandler on Screen*, Stephen Pendo. *It's a Hell of a Life But Not a Bad Living*, Edward Dmytryk. *Faulkner and Film*, Bruce F. Kawin. *Selected Letters of William Faulkner*, ed. Joseph Blotner. *Strangers on a Train*, Patricia Highsmith. *Robert Altman*, Judith M. Kass, and, of course, the works of Chandler himself.

RKO, 20th Century Fox, Paramount, Warner Bros., MGM, United Artists, Avco Embassy, and ITC are the original distributors of the films represented in the book. Thanks to them and to Flashbacks, the Kobal Collection, and the National Film Archive.

Thank you also to the Margaret Herrick Library of the Academy of Motion Picture Arts and Sciences, and the UCLA Library; to Russell Foster and Jill St. Amant; particularly, to Marina Finlay, who typed the manuscript, and Mark Williams, who took the location photographs.

Finally, an appreciative nod to Glenn Goldman, who pointed me in the right direction; to Gwen Feldman, who said yes; and to Don Boyd, whose original support set the whole thing in motion.

A. C.

CHAPTER 1
PROLOGUE

The Transcendence of Ordinariness

There is an inexplicable fascination with what writers do when they are not working, as if it were at these moments that they entered some arcane, rarefied dimension. Raymond Chandler liked to write letters. Thousands of them. He wrote letters to his agent, his publisher, his lawyer, his secretary, fellow writers, friends, journalists, the editors of periodicals to which he contributed, and women in whom he was interested but was too awkward to approach.

Freewheeling in tone, yet stylistically as fastidious as any of his published work, the letters suggest not so much a man revealing himself privately to a circle of people with whom conversation may have proved insufficient as one who wishes to be remembered as a perceptive, amusing, principled crusader, and who ensures that his correspondence reveals those designated aspects of his personality that his presence fails to convey. It was this desire to transcend his own tetchy, neurotic ordinariness that led to the creation of detective fiction's most distinctive and enduring character, Philip Marlowe.

Characteristically, he wrote a letter about him as well. From it we can establish that Marlowe was born in Santa Rosa, California, has always been thirty-eight years old, is slightly over six feet tall, weighs thirteen stone eight, has dark brown hair, brown eyes, will smoke almost any cigarette, drink anything that is not sweet, makes good coffee, plays adequate chess, and likes women. He does not have a secretary.

Raymond Chandler in Los Angeles, 1940. Photograph: Alfred A. Knopf.

Chandler was born in Chicago on July 23, 1888, of a drunkenly violent father and a self-sacrificingly benevolent Irish mother, both non-practicing Quakers. After his parents' divorce, he traveled with his mother to London, where, at the age of eight, he entered the austere matriarchal household of his aunt and attended Dulwich College, a nearby school renowned for its academic thoroughness. From one, he acquired a reverence toward older women; from the other, a confidence in the power of education.

His schooling concluded, a spell in the Admiralty relinquished, and early aspirations as a freelance poet and essayist exhausted, he traveled to America by ship and continued the journey overland to California. Shortly after, with the outbreak of World War I, he went to Canada and enlisted in the Gordon Highlanders. In France, he served with the first division of the Canadian Expeditionary Force and in England with the Royal Flying Corps. Discharged in 1919, he returned to California with his increasingly sick mother and, after a number of temporary jobs—among them, picking apricots and stringing tennis rackets—began working for an oil company.

Two weeks after his mother's death in 1924, Chandler married Pearl Cecily Hurlburt, known as Cissy, already twice married and nearly seventeen years his senior. It was a bizarre, reclusive bond, to last for the remainder of their respective lifetimes. He was clearly embarrassed by the disparity in their ages, but the strength of his emotional attachment eclipsed any potential satisfaction to be derived from fantasies of independence. However many secretaries he chased around the filing cabinets at the Dabney Oil Syndicate, or affairs he later attempted to set in motion when he worked at Paramount, the umbilical cord always led back to Cissy. His own final years following her death in 1954 were despairing to an extreme degree.

He spent much of that time in London—a broken old man, still wearing the white gloves he had once adopted to disguise a skin complaint; nervous, egocentric, remote, self-pitying, drinking heavily, and forever threatening suicide. He was consoled by friends like Natasha Spender, the wife of poet and critic Stephen Spender; Helga Greene, his last literary agent, whom he greatly admired, probably loved, and almost married; and Dilys Powell, who had been among the first British journalists to applaud his work and encourage interest in it. She once found herself defending him in conversation against the sneers of Irwin Shaw and William Saroyan, who were appalled by her championing of a "pulp writer." "It was as if I had advanced Mickey Spillane as a candidate for the Nobel Prize," she recalled.

Miss Powell and her husband, Leonard Russell, who was then the literary editor of the *Sunday Times*, occasionally played host to Chandler, with and without Cissy. "He never talked about his work," she said, "and Cissy never talked about anything. She was like a mother figure, but dressed like a girl and with canary-colored hair. Everyone was always pleased to meet Raymond, although he didn't appear to appreciate it. He was no conversationalist, not even an amusing guest. Toward the end, it got difficult. Even Hamish Hamilton [Chandler's English publisher] got fed up with him dropping his head into the soup plate."

By the late 1920s, Chandler was a director of several oil companies. By 1932, at the age of forty-four, he had no job, the Depression and his own increasingly erratic behavior synchronizing to show him the door. Impressed by such exponents of American detective fiction as Dashiell Hammett and Erle Stanley Gardner, he began writing again. A year later, his first story, *Blackmailers Don't Shoot* (for which he was paid one cent a word), was published in the pulp magazine *Black Mask*, much of whose character had been initiated by Hammett, although Carroll John Daly's private eye Race Williams seems to have had an early start on the style if not the skill—"I squeezed lead and the show was over. He was dead five times before he hit the floor."

Chandler's short-story detectives like Mallory, Carmady, and Dalmas acted as trial runs for the eventual appearance of Philip Marlowe, although an impeccably downbeat investigator of that name (minus the "e") appears in the otherwise undistinguished *Finger Man* (1934). In his celebrated essay *The Simple Art of Murder*, Chandler describes Marlowe's fusion of characteristics without ever referring to him by name: "He must be a complete man and a common man and yet an unusual man. He must be, to use a rather weathered phrase, a man of honor, by instinct, by inevitability, without thought of it, and certainly without saying it . . . He will take no man's money dishonestly and no man's insolence without due and dispassionate revenge. He is a lonely man and his pride is that you will treat him as a proud man or be very sorry you ever saw him. He talks as a man of his age talks, that is, with rude wit, a lively sense of the grotesque, a disgust for sham, and a contempt for pettiness . . . If there were enough like him, I think the world would be a very safe place to live in, and yet not be too dull to be worth living in."

There are some who consider that Marlowe's moral code, despite the self-deprecating manner in which it is invariably expressed, is that of a sentimental, anachronistic dullard. Others, like the writer Michael Mason, view him as a little more than a repressed closet case. Characters in the novels ridicule his chivalry. Dr. Carl Moss in *The High Window* calls him "a shop-soiled Galahad" while Menendez in *The Long Good-Bye* regards him as "Tarzan on a big red scooter."

As easy to dismiss as he is difficult to define, Marlowe reflects the ambivalence of his originator. He is both tough and tender, intrinsically isolated yet selectively sociable, literate but suspicious of culture, poetic yet deflating in his irony. As well as writing detective fiction, Chandler was one of its principal theorists and was perpetually aware of the tightrope he trod between the existing traditions of the medium and his own propensity for sabotage. He wanted "to get murder away from the upper classes, the weekend house party, and the vicar's rose garden and back to the people who are really good at it."

Yet as an educated man who wanted to give detective fiction a status more befitting what he considered to be its worth, Chandler was still unsettled by any whiff of literary ostentation. He enjoyed Ross Macdonald's *The Moving Target* but found the description of a car being "acned with rust" pretentious. Eric Ambler, he felt, allowed himself to be too overtly "intellectual" instead of accepting the premise of "doing what you want to do in a form that the public has learned to accept." As ever, Hammett fell outside his critical butterfly net. "He had style, but his audience didn't know it because it was a language not supposed to be capable of such refinements."

In his own work, Chandler favored a lively American vernacular for dialogue and a classically sound syntax for narrative and descriptive passages, a combination that, for all its intrinsic dangers—one is initially relieved to find that the racketeers in his books are not also part-time etymologists—works with great effectiveness. It was a style he was to employ, with varying degrees of success, on seven novels, two dozen short stories, numerous articles, and enough letters to sink a small ocean liner, all of them revealing differing aspects of their creator's confused, kaleidoscopic character: a miserable bastard, probably a genius.

Los Angeles at night from the Hollywood Hills: the statutory carpet of lights, as immortalized by numerous films (before they built the Holiday Inn).

A Place in the Sun

"God, what an ugly town this has become!" Boris Karloff, playing a gently sardonic old film actor rather like himself in Peter Bogdanovich's film *Targets* (1967), is staring ruefully out of his limousine window at the car showrooms and parking lots of Los Angeles, no longer scars on a landscape he knew differently but now, as far as he is concerned, the landscape itself.

Tod Hackett, the central character in Nathanael West's novel *The Day of the Locust*, is at work on a painting, "The Burning Of Los Angeles": "Across the top, parallel with the frame, he had drawn the burning city, a great bonfire of architectural styles, ranging from Egyptian to Cape Cod colonial. Through the center, winding from left to right, was a long hill street and down it, spilling into the middle foreground, came the mob carrying baseball bats and torches. For the faces of its members, he was using the innumerable sketches he had made of the people who came to California to die; the cultists of all sorts, economic as well as religious, the wave, airplane, funeral, and preview watchers—all those poor devils who can be stirred by the promise of miracles and then only to violence."

Ten years after West but eighteen before Bogdanovich, Raymond Chandler is ruminating, through his intermediary Philip Marlowe in *The Little Sister*, on the city that he helped to immortalize: "I used to like this town. A long time ago. There were trees along Wilshire Boulevard. Beverly Hills was a country town. Westwood was bare hills and lots offering at eleven hundred dollars and no takers. Hollywood was a bunch of frame houses on the inter-urban line. Los Angeles was just a big, dry, sunny place with ugly homes and no style, but good-hearted and peaceful. It had the climate they just yap about now. People used to sleep out on porches. Little groups who thought they were intellectual used to call it the Athens of America. It wasn't that, but it wasn't a neon-lighted slum, either."

Chandler had once liked Los Angeles as much as he had hated Bay City, the flimsy alias by which he identified Santa Monica, then a separate town. More importantly, he had brought it to life in literature, giving it a mythical aspect of which even its inhabitants were unaware. When Marlowe drove around the area to visit the people who had lost someone and wanted him to find them, those who might know their whereabouts, and the web of wickedness that led from one to the other, he invariably traveled through a particular area, along an authentic boulevard, and up a specific street. Chandler always emphasized locations in a manner that continues to provide fascination for students of the city.

It is not a *popular* city in that it is rarely admired by outsiders, many of whom, their prejudice matched by their ignorance, persist in viewing Los Angeles in the most crudely hackneyed way: a sun-kissed joke, a seventy-square-mile sprawl of sybaritic emptiness that, bordered by mountains, desert, and ocean, provides its inhabitants with the almost-constant good weather in which to indulge their preposterous narcissism.

Ultimately, of course, it is snobbery that underlines the resentment. Clive James once made the observation that the hidden assumption behind all the mockery that has ever been aimed at California is that existence is not meant to be that easy. An easy target for mockery— some might go so far as to say that it personifies the place—is the Los Angeles River. Mark Twain, when visiting the West Coast, was amazed by it—the only river, he concluded, where one could fall in and come out dusty. Formed by a confluence of creeks in the San Fernando Valley, it is fundamentally a fifty-mile-long drainage ditch— lined with concrete since floods in 1938 revealed an inability to keep its shape—that eventually emits a derisory trickle into the Pacific at San Pedro Bay near Long Beach. You could drive a car along it and only get a puncture from a discarded bottle.

In truth, Los Angeles is the most rapidly growing city in the western world, which in turn makes it one of the most complex. It feels above all like a city of the future, a blueprint for what many cities will become in the next century. As befits a transient, segregated coalition of communities, it is a place of paradoxes, and of extremes of behavior. Oscillating between vanity and self-destruction, people there have a talent for living in the present. They are obsessively concerned with appearance, exercise, redemption, and immortality—bespoken by the mushrooming abundance of plastic surgeons, personal trainers, addiction support groups, and low-fat dieticians in the area—yet they take immense quantities of drugs. Most forms of self-gratification can be ordered on the telephone.

"In place of a sense of belonging," *Playboy* once observed, in the days when one could still swim there, "Los Angeles offers a day at the beach." Extremes of freedom and regimentation are in constant evidence. It has some of the most distinguished twentieth-century architecture in the world but encourages little interest in it. Its predominantly Hispanic history, beginning with that of the city itself, is a part of its pulse, yet few Anglos—themselves a minority now—have the curiosity to learn the language. It is one of the richest cities in the world, but it is also, palpably, one of the poorest.

The dreamy resourcefulness that attracted many people to Los Angeles in the first place remains in the architecture. There are buildings that, not content with stopping you in your tracks, then nail your feet to the ground. Some of the better-known ones include a bottling plant—occupying an entire block of an otherwise undistinguished downtown industrial area—with the exterior of an ocean liner and portholes for windows; hot dog and donut stands designed, in a

The Bradbury Building, where Marlowe has his office in **Marlowe** (1969).

perfect fusion of form and function, to represent the shape of the food being sold; a recording-company office with a ninety-two-foot phonograph needle on its roof; a movie theater masquerading as a Chinese pagoda, with Swiss chalets and "old" English castles nestling amid the comic architectural melting pot in the hills behind. Ideas adapted to the needs of a new environment with roots in the old, all subordinated to an extravagant sense of fantasy.

With the exception of the prodigious Bradbury Building (whose discreet Renaissance exterior conceals one of the most arresting amalgams of brick, marble, tile, wood, and cast iron in the world—all illuminated by a huge skylight), most of the impressive constructions, as befits the city's origin as an Hispanic colony in 1769, are Spanish Colonial Revival, a style that, as Reyner Banham remarked in *Los An-*

Union Station, used as a location in **Marlowe** (1969) and by Chandler himself in **The Little Sister** and **Playback**, is like a California mission . . .

geles, his outstanding book about the growth of the city, "makes both ancestral and environmental sense."

Union Station, used as a location by Chandler in *The Little Sister* and *Playback,* is like a California mission housing an Art Deco social club. One sits in a carved wood-and-leather seat in the large waiting room, listening to music emitted from speakers that resemble the public-address system of a Thirties' dance hall, taking a leisurely walk around the Moorish patios between reveries. It transforms waiting for a train into an activity of time-suspended ease. The station opened in May 1939 with festivities that lasted two days. Even the trains were applauded. The first one out, not seen by the public, was a Paramount special to promote the film *Union Pacific* on a 10,000-mile jaunt around the country. Now the movie stars who used to abandon the Super Chief at Pasadena to avoid the crowds at Union Station travel only by private jet.

Initially, however, the decline of rail travel can be attributed to

. . . housing an Art Deco social club.

freeways, which set in motion the Californian obsession with personal mobility. In Joan Didion's *Play It As It Lays*, the central character spends a whole month, beginning at no later than ten each morning, driving on the freeways in the fast lane with the radio playing, keeping on the passenger seat a hard-boiled egg that she can shell and eat at seventy miles per hour.

Multiply one extremist with an exhaust pipe and a hard-boiled egg by several million and the result is immense atmospheric pollution. Acted on by sunlight, of which Southern California has always had plenty, it creates the corrosive irritant of smog, which by the beginning of the next millennium will have acquired almost as long a history as London's pea-souper fogs of the early twentieth century, with one significant difference: the smog in Los Angeles will still be there. "Angelenos were shocked to discover," observed Reyner Banham, "that it was their favorite toy that was fouling up their greatest asset."

The most haunting film to have used the city as both a character and a canvas prophesies, with the benefit of hindsight, that its growth will also be its undoing. In *Chinatown* (1974), Jack Nicholson plays a private detective not unlike Marlowe except that he specializes in matrimonial and divorce work, a field completely alien to his predecessor. Unlike Marlowe, he has few reservations about hitting a woman if it prompts the desired confession. "I'm not in business to be loved," he declares wearily, "but I *am* in business." While doing a seemingly routine investigation of adultery that might involve the chief engineer of the Water and Power Board, he uncovers a network of corruption on a level far beyond anything he had imagined. Wealthy tyrants are pushing farmers off their parched land, buying it for a pittance under the pseudonyms of recently deceased residents of an old people's resthome, and then having it irrigated illegally.

Chinatown is an original screenplay by Robert Towne, although it is closer to Chandler's novels in its mood and range of concerns than anything he ever contributed to the cinema. In effect, it is the screenplay he *should* have written. Towne reflected: "I can remember L.A. before World War II, when it was an entirely different place from what it is now. As I grew older, I realized that the city had a kind of pastel beauty that would soon be lost forever, and that filled me with a sense of loss and longing and sadness. I think *Chinatown* is really about the growth and destruction of the city. To me, they're the same thing. Growth has always been considered good, and nowhere has it been considered more good than here. Unlike some countries, where people have been more aware of their natural resources and husband them much more carefully, here it has always seemed as if our resources were infinite. It's just like cancer. Uncontrolled growth.

"I read an article about Chandler and L.A. and it occurred to me that those places he described were still there and hadn't changed, and a movie would be a chance of capturing the city for the last time before they pile all that stuff under completely. Then I read *Southern California Country* by Carey McWilliams. I was particularly interested in a section on water in the Owens Valley and the rape of the valley that had gone on to bring water to L.A. Things took shape from there. I ended up doing a story about a man who raped the land and his daughter, at least one of them in the name of progress. Chandler was more of an inspiration in terms of his feeling for the city than anything else . . . When corruption is that pervasive, you really can't catch anybody. When it's so huge that they can't punish it, they reward it. The names of these guys end up on plaques in City Hall."

Movie Detectives

The detective in *Chinatown,* and in its ill-fated sequel, *The Two Jakes* (1990), is called Jake Gittes, but his name is not important. Outwardly composed, but inwardly disheveled—like some bruised, tarnished variation on the folkloric All-American hero—his life, like that of most screen sleuths, is essentially a solitary one, as befits a hired snooper parrying the resentment of those in whose lives he necessarily interferes.

Detectives in the cinema are nearly as old as the medium itself, and equally abiding. Ever since Conan Doyle's deductive eccentric first applied his unerring logic on film at the turn of the century in *Sherlock Holmes Baffled,* movies have continually provided a backdrop for investigators of all temperaments and working methods, from the cheerfully debonair Philo Vance (adapted with metronomic regularity from S.S. Van Dine's novels between 1929 and 1947 and portrayed by no less than ten actors, most notably William Powell) to the tiresomely pugnacious Mike Hammer.

Jack Nicholson as J. J. Gittes in **Chinatown** (1974): outwardly composed, but inwardly disheveled.

It was a matter of routine that detectives should have their own series if the films could be made at a sufficiently low budget. The actor who played the detective was encouraged to do so for as long as possible, but was usually easy to replace. There were starchy, impassive Orientals like Charlie Chan (Warner Oland or Sidney Toler), Mr. Moto (Peter Lorre), and Mr. Wong (Boris Karloff); quasi-moralistic crusaders, bordering on the fascistic, such as Bulldog Drummond (Jack Buchanan, Ronald Colman and numerous others); nosy old spinsters like Miss Marple, whom Agatha Christie might almost have written for Margaret Rutherford, or Hildegarde Withers, whom Stuart Palmer could have modeled on Edna May Oliver; and resolute bachelors such as Rex Stout's orchid-loving Nero Wolfe, initially starring Edward Arnold, who had already played several other detectives and would go on to more.

Each studio developed its own series. Torchy Blaine, a female newspaper reporter securing stories through detection work, was invented by Warners, who also exploited Nancy Drew—from books by Carolyn Keene—in four films about a teenage girl who follows up on dubious official verdicts with the help of her lawyer father. Jonathan Latimer provided Universal with the raw material for three Bill Crane films. Columbia had the Crime Doctor and Lone Wolf series. Fox favored Brett Halliday's Michael Shayne while RKO, when the feud with Leslie Charteris over their treatment of the Saint had developed to tedious lengths, quickly assimilated the Saint's characteristics and changed his name to the Falcon. Neither RKO nor Fox cared where they acquired the source material for their detectives, as evidenced by the speed with which they tailored Raymond Chandler's second and third Philip Marlowe novels to the idiosyncrasies of their own franchise characters, the Falcon and Michael Shayne.

Single experiments like MGM's *Haunted Honeymoon* (1940), in which Robert Montgomery does a satisfactory impersonation of Dorothy L. Sayers' Lord Peter Wimsey, usually indicated a studio's lack of confidence in a character, while the absence of any films based on Erle Stanley Gardner books after *The Case of the Stuttering Bishop* (1937) is explained by the author's distrust of Hollywood, to which he refused to license any further material, before eventually submitting to CBS radio in the 1940s and the corresponding TV network a decade later.

With the Continental Op in his novels *Red Harvest* and *The Dain Curse*, Dashiell Hammett, himself a former investigator for the Pinkerton agency in San Francisco, more or less invented the private detective in fiction. "I see him," Hammett wrote of his hero, "as a little man going forward day after day through mud and blood and deceit—as callous and brutal and cynical as necessary—toward a dim goal, with nothing to push or pull him to it except that he's been hired to reach it." Hammett's San Francisco was never as seductively evoked as Chandler's Los Angeles, but he provided Chandler with his departure point much in the same way that John Huston's movie of Hammett's *The Maltese Falcon* (1941)—which consummately brought to life the labyrinthine mystery surrounding a black bird and the flashy undesirables in pursuit of it—set the tone for a decade of private-eye films. Despite Sam Spade's brazen opportunism and comparative amorality—he has been having an affair with his partner's wife and accepts retainers from opposing factions—Chandler would have been proud of a line such as the one that Humphrey Bogart casually tosses at Elisha Cook Jr. following a colorful display of tetchiness: "The cheaper the crook, the gaudier the patter."

The only successful immediate successor to Marlowe was Mickey Spillane's Mike Hammer, but—with any suggestion of charm or integrity obfuscated by a general air of cheerless, bellicose Commie-hunting—he was little more than a below-stairs Bulldog Drummond. Understandably, he has prompted no interesting movie adaptations except for Robert Aldrich's remarkable *Kiss Me Deadly* (1955), whose distinctiveness had little to do with Spillane.

The only film to feature John D. MacDonald's Travis McGee is *Darker Than Amber* (1970) with Rod Taylor, toward the end of his inexplicable period of popularity, as the detective. There have also been movie adaptations of Ross Macdonald's first two Lew Archer novels, *The Moving Target* and *The Drowning Pool*. Archer is Marlowe a generation later—divorced, acrimonious, literate, principled—adrift in the same seedily picturesque Southern California. Like Marlowe, Archer tends to have high-life clients with low-life connections, and he takes little prompting to lapse into soliloquies about himself, other people, and the world.

Archer became *Harper* (1966) after a title change (from *The Moving Target*, which it retained in the U.K.) to accommodate Paul

Paul Newman as Lew Harper in **The Moving Target** (1966): the perfect Marlowe-that-never-was.

Newman's superstition—following *The Hustler* (1961) and *Hud* (1963)—that the initial letter H amalgamated, in about equal measures, the approval of critics and the sound of cash registers.

The plot is archetypical Chandler: a rich invalid, whose skittish daughter likes to dance on the diving board by the family pool, wants her husband found. Harper is cool, charming, insolent, laconic, inquisitive. "The bottom is loaded with nice people," he remarks at one point. "Only cream and bastards rise."

"What do you want?" asks his estranged wife when he knocks at her door one night.

"A few kind words."

"What else?"

"Anything I can get." The following morning he abandons her again, prompting her to describe his work, which has clearly come between them in the past, as "just an infinitely lingering disease." *The Drowning Pool* (1975) transfers the novel's action from California to Louisiana, gaining in novelty what it loses in atmosphere, and retains the presence of Newman, who—when his suit has avoided a visit to the dry cleaners and the camera is not paying fawningly disproportionate attention to his blue eyes—remains the perfect Marlowe-that-never-was.

Since the Forties, practically every film about a private detective has appropriated something from Raymond Chandler in one way or another, from the conspicuous plot borrowings of *Tony Rome* (1967) and *Lady in Cement* (1968)—which assume respectively the outlines of *The Big Sleep* and *Farewell, My Lovely*—to the broodingly downbeat mood of Arthur Penn's compelling *Night Moves* (1975) and the shrill pastiche of *Dead Men Don't Wear Plaid* (1982).

While the past two decades have produced several contemporary homages to hardboiled literature and *noir* cinema—outstandingly, Stephen Frears' cool, playful variation (with Donald Westlake) on Jim Thompson's *The Grifters* (1990)—the period detective movie has nearly disappeared. Elmer Bernstein, whose music for *The Grifters* helps to reinforce the film's sinister buoyancy, also scored Carl Franklin's *Devil in a Blue Dress* (1995), the tone of whose opening narration ("It was summer 1948, and I needed money") reveals its unmistakable genre pedigree. Based on the novel by Walter Mosley about his reluctant private detective, Easy Rawlins (a flawless Denzel Washington), as impenetrably plotted and eccentrically populated as Chandler, and featuring an outstanding re-creation of post-war Los Angeles, it is a confident, pleasure-giving film, full of mood and texture.

But the two movies that, in their different ways, most evocatively pay tribute to the Chandler legacy are Lawrence Kasdan's *Body Heat* (1981) and Ridley Scott's *Blade Runner* (1982). *Body Heat* has the traditional *noir* cocktail—murder, lust, greed, betrayal—poured into the customary tumblers—sunlight through shutters, shadows, neon, night fogs. A vintage potion owing a considerable debt to *Double Indemnity*, it somehow manages to be completely timeless: we could be in the mid-Forties, although we know we are not. *Blade Runner* is a spellbinding, highly influential amalgam of pulp fiction and high tech, a vision of Los Angeles in the twenty-first century, when the mean streets are full of rain and steam, and detectives hunt down robots in human form. The particularly Chandleresque narration was removed for the director's-cut reissue of the film in 1992, but its resonance remains.

Those who do not attempt to sanctify Chandler often seek to subvert him. Such an attempt—lightweight, but with a dash of Hammett, too—is *The Big Fix*, written by Roger L. Simon in 1973 and adapted by him as a screenplay for a movie with Richard Dreyfuss six years later. In it, Los Angeles investigator Moses Wine, whose ex-wife lives with a yogi, gets the knock on the door while smoking a hash pipe and listening to Stevie Wonder on headphones.

Evidently, there comes a time in every private eye's life when the office bottle and the sound of the traffic will no longer do.

Warm Weather, Easy Money

In 1943, Raymond Chandler began work at Paramount, earning a handsome weekly salary—a little under half of what he had received two years earlier for the film rights to *Farewell, My Lovely.* "If my books had been any worse," he told Charles Morton of *The Atlantic Monthly,* "I should not have been invited to Hollywood. If they had been any better, I should not have come."

Many prominent novelists and playwrights, a large proportion of them European exiles, had preceded him to this Los Angeles suburb at the foot of the Santa Monica mountains, tantalized by the prospect of warm weather and easy money. P.G. Wodehouse took a screenwriting job at MGM in 1931 and received a substantial income for contributing little more than his presence, an experience that provided him with ample material for short stories. John O'Hara made a good deal of money polishing dialogue and, later, writing screenplays. Dashiell Hammett, on the other hand, derived little profit or satisfaction from his protracted stint, while writers such as Christopher Isherwood, Aldous Huxley, John Steinbeck, Dorothy Parker, Robert Benchley, Lillian Hellman, Clifford Odets, William Faulkner, and F. Scott Fitzgerald, all of them familiar with a studio paycheck, spent much of their overlapping time knocking back the drinks in a booth at Musso & Frank and amusing each other with stories about their employers. Hollywood, it seemed, had hired them for their talents and then proceeded to waste them by placing them under the supervision of bureaucratic Philistines.

For Fitzgerald, who lacked the pragmatism of some of the others, it was a particularly wretched experience. When he arrived in the film capital for the third time in 1937, he was in debt and greatly in need of a boost to his confidence. The first visit, ten years earlier, had seemed so different. In a letter to his daughter Scottie, he described the scene: "At that time I had been acknowledged for several years as the top American writer both seriously and, as far as prices went, popularly. Hollywood made a big fuss over us and the ladies all looked very beautiful to a man of thirty. Total result—a great time and no work." On the second occasion he was hired by Irving Thalberg, later the model for Monroe Stahr in *The Last Tycoon*, to write

Chandler worked for four studios. Paramount was the only one he liked.

the screenplay for a Jean Harlow vehicle, *Red Headed Woman,* but discovered that his script was being sabotaged. It was later completed by, and credited to, Anita Loos. On his return, he was assigned to adapt Erich Maria Remarque's *Three Comrades.* He finished the work, only to be informed that he needed a collaborator, E.E. Paramore, with whom he argued incessantly. Most novelists do not work well with partners, a system that Hollywood cherished, as Chandler was to find to his cost several years later.

From then on, it was a despairing downhill ride for Fitzgerald. He wrote screenplays for *Marie Antoinette, The Women,* and *Madame Curie,* but none of them was used. He was one of the innumerable dialogue polishers on *Gone with the Wind,* but this was routine work in which he could take little pride. His MGM contract expired. During his twilight years in Hollywood, he wrote *The Pat Hobby Stories* for *Esquire*: wry, rueful, lightly humorous tales about about a down-at-heel middle-aged scriptwriter who, "being of the older Hollywood, understood their jokes, their vanities, their social system with its swift fluctuations." Soon after, while expanding on the same themes in *The Last Tycoon*, he died.

Chandler worked for four studios, and Paramount was the only one he liked. "They do somehow maintain the country-club atmosphere there to some extent," he wrote to Carl Brandt, his agent at the time. "At the writers' table at Paramount I heard some of the best wit I've ever heard in my life." Melvin Frank was, with his partner, Norman Panama, one of the presiding lives of the party: "At Paramount, there were two big tables where the writers had lunch. Ours was the Panama and Frank table, mainly comedy writers but really anyone who came in. We used to play a match game. Someone held between one and four matches in his hand, and people had to guess the amount. Those who didn't guess correctly had to pay for everyone's lunch. We did that with Chandler. My contact with him was restricted to hearing stories about him and Billy Wilder, having lunch, playing match games, and occasionally running into him in the toilet. He made good money at Paramount, more than many of us who had been there for a long time. Most of the big novelists generally had contempt for Hollywood. They would come in, pick up a lot of money for a job, and then go and do their creative writing. I met William Faulkner in the toilet as well, although that was at Warners. My partner, Norman Panama, was using an electric razor, and Faulkner, who had never seen one before, asked if he could use it."

While Melvin Frank kept meeting famous writers in the toilet, Chandler merely kept changing his mind. Three years before his letter praising Hollywood writers and their sense of humor, he wrote an article for *The Atlantic Monthly* dismissing them as a bunch of acquiescent blockheads: "They are, to put it bluntly, a pretty dreary lot of hacks, and most of them know it, and they take their kicks and their salaries and try to be reasonably grateful to an industry that permits them to live much more opulently than they could live anywhere else."

Finally, it was just a matter of having an opinion. To disapprove of Hollywood was somehow correct. To commend it was satisfyingly perverse. Above all, there were letters to be written.

CHAPTER 2

THE EARLY FRANCHISES

The Falcon Takes Over, Time to Kill

Four years after he had introduced a smooth, sardonic sleuth called the Saint into his third novel, *Meet the Tiger*, in 1928, Leslie Charteris moved to Hollywood and began working in the Writers Building at Paramount. When his own country of residence changed, so did the Saint's. Instead of outwitting Scotland Yard in his gentlemanly pursuit of criminals, he now confused the New York police. He had probably not yet heard of the LAPD.

Always in search of material that might prompt a successful series, RKO purchased the film rights to *The Saint in New York*, the first of his translatlantic adventures, and the sequence was under way in 1938, with Louis Hayward as the debonair dick. For the next, *The Saint Strikes Back* (1939), they borrowed George Sanders from 20th Century Fox, where he was under contract, and continued to employ him in *The Saint in London* (1939) and *The Saint's Double Trouble* (1940). To say that Charteris did not approve of the films would be an extravagant understatement. He loathed them. From the moment RKO had been presumptuous enough to choose its own Saint, he persistently objected to miscasting, to liberties taken with his plots, and to alterations made to his characters. RKO was not amused by Charteris's exuberant protests, and to shut him up they offered him the opportunity to revise Frank Fenton and Lynn Root's screenplay for *The Saint Takes Over* (1940), to which he made little discernible difference, and to provide the story outline for *The Saint in Palm Springs,* Sanders' last film in the role. Charteris was unassuaged by the studio's open-handedness. The death rattle of the series was already audible.

RKO needed a new detective. Not being a company to hold back when there was money to be made, they simply changed the name of the central character from the Saint to the Falcon. A short story, *Gay Falcon* by Michael Arlen, was found and George Sanders retained to play him, which he did with the same bored, nonchalant charm he had brought to his portrayal of the Saint, and which he appeared to apply to his life generally. Charteris's by-now public hostility materialized in the form of a lawsuit against RKO for "unfair competition." They settled out of court and RKO sold an unreleased Saint stiff to Republic, partly to recover their costs but mainly to wash their corporate hands of the entire grisly business.

As there were no Falcon stories as such, apart from the one that provided the central figure, material was adapted from other sources. In July 1941, Raymond Chandler signed a contract with RKO that gave the studio the film rights to his second novel, *Farewell, My Lovely,* for $2000, an agreement he later blamed on "almost unparalleled stupidity on the part of my New York agent." No doubt he would have been incensed further by the discovery that the sum in question was well under half of what Michael Arlen had received for his original short story, and less than Arlen was paid per film for the continued use of the Falcon character.

The Falcon Takes Over (1942) was the third film in the series (after *The Gay Falcon* and *A Date With the Falcon,* both released during the previous year). Fenton and Root were assigned to modify the convoluted narrative of Chandler's *Farewell, My Lovely* to fit the requirements of the Falcon formula while Irving Reis, who had directed the first two pictures, stayed on to do another. Wendy Barrie, the leading lady in them, did not and was replaced by Lynn Bari—like Sanders, on loan from Fox.

The most distinctive feature of *The Falcon Takes Over,* a film not overly endowed with them, is how little it has to do with Raymond Chandler. It is set in New York, where the Falcon resides in an elegant town house, attended by his valet, favoring evening dress and

A would-be reporter (Lynn Bari), an imperturbable amateur sleuth (George Sanders), and a long-suffering stooge (Allen Jenkins) in **The Falcon Takes Over** (1942).

As an indication of their respective positions on the ladder of police life, Inspector O'Hara (James Gleason, left) has the brim of his hat turned down while his bullied blunderer of a partner (Edward Gargan, second from right) has his up.

sporting a suave air of world-weary Anglophilia. His long-suffering stooge Goldie Locke, enthusiastically played by Allen Jenkins, provides the statutory comic relief. There are several policemen, none of them corrupt, to disapprove of the Falcon's interference in their case. Some confine themselves to folkloric exclamations like "Open in the name of the law!"; others, like the blundering Inspector O'Hara (James Gleason), are compulsive punsters. "Make a choice," he in-

Moose Malloy (Ward Bond) has that remote, obsessed look that suggests that the pursuit of pleasure is not among his priorities.

forms Goldie in the middle of an ineffectual interrogation, "sing or Sing-Sing." As an indication of their respective positions on the ladder of police life, O'Hara has the brim of his hat turned down while his bullied blunderer of a partner (Edward Gargan) has his up.

The title sequence—its buoyantly whimsical music score over the outline of a cartoon dandy in overcoat, top hat, and cane, with a smoke ring spiralling above him—reveals the film's playful mood just as the first set of the corner of New York's 7th Avenue and 52nd Street (the entire movie was shot in a studio) bespeaks its minimal budget.

Escaping from jail after serving five years (curiously, almost certainly unintentionally, three less than in the novel) on a false murder charge, Moose Malloy—played by Ward Bond, who had recently been one of the detectives in Huston's *The Maltese Falcon*—swears revenge on his former girlfriend Velma, who betrayed him and has since changed her name and identity. He has that remote, obsessed look that suggests that the pursuit of pleasure is not among his priorities. This is confirmed when he accosts a bystander outside a club where Velma had once worked, and is further underlined when he throws the doorman aside, dispatches the head waiter across the room, and breaks the manager's neck. Clearly, he has some kind of a social problem.

Malloy does not employ the Falcon, as his literary counterpart does Marlowe, because the Falcon is not a professional detective; he is a gentleman investigator, an imperturbable amateur sleuth, and, therefore, not the kind of person into whose company the easily perturbed Moose might stray. Despite having supposedly retired from detective work, and to the evident displeasure of the police department, he is called in to help—languid, detached, amused, leading one to wonder with what ease Sanders might have ambled through the James Bond films had the series been started two decades earlier.

In pursuit of Moose, the Falcon visits Jessie Florian, the widow of the club's former owner, at her house in Washington Lane, Brooklyn, constructed on a soundstage as a country road. Moose is about to leave and, in his expressively bovine way, shows some displeasure at seeing the Falcon, who feigns drunkenness. Mrs. Florian, in the prototype of the dressing gown that was to grace the subsequent adaptations of *Farewell, My Lovely*, is an irascible old harridan who finds the Falcon's charms highly resistible. At the conclusion of his attempted inquisition, she throws a bottle of whisky at him and it smashes against a door. "Now you won't get your deposit back," he retorts reprovingly.

Lindsay Marriott, played with oleaginous precision and a pencil moustache by Hans Conried, engages the Falcon as a bodyguard when he delivers the ransom money for the return of a necklace belonging to a rich female predator he knows. The place of exchange is not a canyon near Malibu but a cemetery outside New York where the steam rises as if in anticipation of some sudden resurrection. Marriott shoots the Falcon only to be gunned down, rather more terminally, by someone else. A would-be reporter from Morgan, Minnesota, Anne Riordan (Lynn Bari) appears on the scene and stays. There are none of the more obvious plot adjustments evident in *Murder, My Sweet*, the next film adaptation of *Farewell, My Lovely*, in which Velma becomes Anne's stepmother; nor are there any of its drugged reveries, sudden violence, or random menace. Instead, one finds that the villainous Jules Amthor has been transformed into a bogus fortuneteller in a turban.

George Sanders: languid, detached, amused—leading one to wonder with what ease he might have ambled through the James Bond films had they been started two decades earlier.

The villainous Jules Amthor (Turhan Bey), transformed into a bogus fortuneteller in a turban.

The Falcon Takes Over understands its function and performs it. Competently and agreeably featherweight, it subordinates any consideration for rhythm and mood to the uniform requirements of the six-reel potboiler made for nothing in no time. For all its bloodless vacuity, and its complete disregard for even the spirit of Chandler's taut, atmospheric prose, it somehow attains its modest purpose. The *Motion Picture Herald* of May 9, 1942, informed its readers that the film had been previewed at the Pantages Theatre in Hollywood, "where a ripple of chuckles sweeping the audience at regular intervals indicated pleased acceptance."

The Falcon finds the identity-changed Velma (Helen Gilbert).

Apparently immune to pleased acceptance, Sanders was unwilling to appear in any more Falcon films. RKO, anxious to exploit its modest but lucrative franchise, persuaded him to do another on the understanding that it would co-star his brother Tom Conway, whose career he wished to help. In accordance with the elevated thinking that characterized the series, it was called *The Falcon's Brother*.

RKO had not been alone in seeking a new detective figure for their profitable B-movie output. Fox stumbled over some routine but robust thrillers by Brett Halliday and was attracted to the novels' resident private eye, Michael Shayne, who, in comparison with the supercilious Falcon, was a paragon of straight-shooting simplicity. Lloyd Nolan played him, initially on a one-picture agreement, in *Michael Shayne, Private Detective* (1940), which was sufficiently successful at

Michael Shayne (Lloyd Nolan, right) in **Time to Kill** (1942): a paragon of straight-shooting simplicity.

Shayne, facing another gun in pocket.

A tyrannical dowager (Ethel Griffiths) and her secretary (Heather Angel).

the box-office to prompt Fox to place him under contract. At the same time, as with the Falcon films, it was decided to draw storylines from whatever source could best provide them. Consequently, *Sleepers West, Dressed to Kill, Blue White and Perfect* (all 1941), *The Man Who Wouldn't Die, Just Off Broadway,* and *Time to Kill* (1942) all employed material that, in everything but the presence of its central character, had nothing to do with Brett Halliday, whose involvement was restricted to watching the growth of his bank account.

Fox had paid $3500 for the film rights to *The High Window,* Chandler's third novel, and used it as the departure point for *Time to Kill,* the seventh and last of a series that was briefly resurrected in the late Forties. Producer Sol Wurtzel hired Clarence Upson Young to condense Chandler's labyrinthine plot and Herbert I. Leeds to direct the result.

Michael Shayne is ordinary, honorable, and a combative bargainer, despite being referred to as "a gay debonair sleuth" in a synopsis clearly written by someone who has his detectives confused. He is neither as ostentatiously correct as Philo Vance nor as gratuitously grumpy as, say, the Continental Op. His only bad habit is that he is given to visiting apartments a few minutes after there has been a homicide. Lloyd Nolan portrays him perfectly: brisk and purposeful, yet amusing and engaging.

In the opening scene, Shayne is viewed speaking on the telephone from behind his shoes on the table, a shot so pleasing to director Leeds that it is repeated ten minutes later. Shayne is asked to drive his Buick to 1439 Dresden Avenue in Pasadena, the residence of Mrs. Murdock, a tyrannical dowager with the tongue of a bad-tempered lizard. Having first met her extremely nervous secretary, Merle (an effectively agitated performance from Heather Angel) in a drawer of whose desk he notices a gun, Shayne is asked to recover a rare coin, the Brasher Doubloon, which has been stolen from Mrs. Murdock's late husband's collection. Mrs. Murdock believes it was taken by Linda Conquest, who is stupid enough to have married her son Leslie but smart enough to have left him. Leslie, who occasionally affects a smoking jacket, has the wit of a small filing cabinet. When visited by him for information, Shayne greets him with a line that Chandler himself might have wished he had written: "Business is really picking up when the worm comes to the early bird."

Indeed, Clarence Upson Young provides Shayne with an avalanche of epigrams that confidently trip off his tongue. "I've got good news for the old lioness," he remarks when calling for Mrs. Murdock. "Pry her loose from her raw meat and put her on the phone." Later in the film, he has reason to knock out Leslie, which he accomplishes by throwing a telephone receiver at him. When the police arrive and require an explanation, he informs them, impeccably deadpan, that Leslie "had a little headache so he's taking a nap."

Despite its cheerfully modest intentions, *Time to Kill*—which, at sixty-one minutes, clocks in at two breathless minutes less than *The Falcon Takes Over*—is superior in every way to Fox's supposedly more "authentic" remake, *The Brasher Doubloon*, five years later. It is more loyal to Chandler, despite deleting the occasional interesting sub-plot (Merle, for example, does not like men to touch her), more convincingly witty, more thoroughly likeable. Even its old-fashioned wrap-up finale—in which Shayne produces a photograph that proves Merle did not push Mr. Murdock out of a window, as everyone including herself suspects—reveals its counterpart in *Doubloon* as the piece of pointless artifice that it is. Indeed, *Time to Kill's* only element of imaginative fabrication is to make the villainess choke to death on a T-bone steak.

Time to Kill: cheerful, modest, breathless.

For Chandler, whose increasing status was reflected in the speed with which Philip Marlowe replaced the Falcon and Michael Shayne, Hollywood's golden index finger beckoned. Little realizing the consequences, he acceded.

CHAPTER 3

HELLO TO HOLLYWOOD

Double Indemnity

"The screenwriter is an employee without power
or decision over the uses of his own craft, without
ownership of it, and, however extravagantly paid,
almost without honor for it."
Raymond Chandler, writing in *The Atlantic Monthly*,
November 1945

In the summer of 1943, Raymond Chandler was on the weary side
of fifty-five. It was ten years since his first short story had been
published, four since his debut as a novelist, and he was beginning to acquire the rudiments of a reputation as a writer.

A producer at Paramount named Joseph Sistrom, looking through
some back issues of *Liberty* magazine (whose most endearing idio-
syncrasy was that it printed a recommended reading time for each
story) came across a serialization of *Double Indemnity*, a novella by
James M. Cain (reading time two hours, fifty minutes, seven seconds)
about a bored housewife, a hungry insurance salesman, and their
scheme to murder her husband, on whom they have taken out an
accident policy. Cain had already used a similar plot in his first novel,
The Postman Always Rings Twice—published in 1934 and filmed four
times—by having a bored waitress and a hungry drifter scheming to

murder *her* husband. Both books were reputedly inspired by the notorious killing in 1927 of Albert Snyder by his wife, Ruth, and her lover, Judd Gray, for his insurance.

A former journalist, bringing to his novels a vividly condensed sense of detail, Cain arrived in Los Angeles in 1931 to work as a screenwriter and soon began to chronicle his surroundings in books. His three celebrated novels set in the area—*Double Indemnity, The Postman Always Rings Twice,* and *Mildred Pierce* (which was to become a movie vehicle for Joan Crawford)—combine superior storytelling with a real feeling for the victims of the period, their pursuit of passion and prosperity in collision with their Depression anxieties. Sistrom was impressed.

So was Billy Wilder, who finished it in fifty-eight minutes. The author of numerous scripts in Germany and several in Hollywood, Wilder had already written (in partnership with Charles Brackett) and directed two films for Paramount, *The Major and the Minor* and *Five Graves to Cairo.* Anticipating a further collaboration with Brackett, Wilder enthusiastically gave him *Double Indemnity* and awaited his response. Brackett hated it: he refused to work on material so completely deficient in moral atonement. Words were exchanged, most of them by a splenetic Wilder. Sistrom asked Cain to help, but found him busy on another screenplay. Then he remembered a writer in what he considered a similar tradition: Raymond Chandler. (There is some irony in this, as after the publication of his third novel, *The High Window* in 1943, Chandler had sent a letter to his publisher, Alfred Knopf, in which James Cain is summarily dismissed: "Everything he touches smells like a billygoat," wrote Chandler. "He is every kind of writer I detest, a *faux naif,* a Proust in greasy overalls, a dirty little boy with a piece of chalk and a board fence and nobody looking. Such people are the offal of literature, not because they write about dirty things but because they do it in a dirty way.")

Sistrom encouraged Wilder to read Chandler's *The Big Sleep,* which he did. Invigorated by its poetic toughness, Wilder was also excited to find that Chandler understood Los Angeles so well, and the kind of treacherous instincts that propelled its darker undercurrents.

Chandler was traced to 6520 Drexel Avenue in West Hollywood, to where he and his wife, Cissy, had recently moved. Despite many years of living in and around Los Angeles, he had never set foot in a film studio and had no idea of where Paramount was located. Sistrom gave him instructions on how to drive there.

When he met him, Wilder was astonished. As far as he could recall, he had not asked the casting department to send over a schoolmaster. Expecting a witty, combative character with the shoulders of a stevedore and a handshake like a pair of industrial pliers, he was instead confronted by a nervous, pallid academic, wearing a sports jacket with patches on the elbows and smoking a pipe.

In the course of the initial discussion, Chandler proposed his terms. He would require $150 a week while writing the screenplay, which he anticipated would take him no longer than a month. Sistrom, his negotiating technique turned on its head by the modesty of Chandler's demands, informed him that he would be paid a weekly salary of $750 for as long as he was working on the picture. He would also be provided with an office in Paramount's Writers Building and a secretary.

Wilder and Chandler parted company for the weekend, mutually bewildered and fearing the worst. It seemed unlikely that this egregious Middle European misanthrope with a riding crop could co-exist with a diffident novelist of scholarly leanings. On the following Monday, Wilder arrived with a few notes, Chandler with the beginning of a punctiliously detailed and descriptive screenplay. Disappointed by Chandler's failure to understand the procedure, the *etiquette*, of co-writing a film, Wilder reminded him that it was a collaboration that would take as long as was necessary. Chandler listened silently. The prospects were not promising.

Wilder once described Chandler as "a naive, sweet, warm man" whose only liability was not having worked with a partner before. Elsewhere, both have alluded to their association in more dismissive terms. Chandler, writing to his British publisher Hamish Hamilton in 1950, declared that "working with Billy Wilder on *Double Indemnity* was an agonizing experience and has probably shortened my life, but I learned from it about as much about screenwriting as I am capable of learning, which is not very much."

So, the two grudging collaborators shut themselves away and began work. Wilder paced the room like an agitated interrogator; Chandler sat in a chair surrounded by the clouds of smoke from his pipe. Wilder swished around a Malacca cane as he prowled and made frequent visits to the bathroom as a refuge from Chandler's increasingly obvious disapproval. Wilder wore hats in the office, to which Chandler objected, feeling that it suggested imminent departure. He would sometimes ask Chandler to open a window or pull the venetian blinds. He took long phone calls from women during working hours. He did not say "please" when requesting something.

One day, Chandler failed to show up for work. He did not appear the next day either. On the third morning he was in Sistrom's office with a list of complaints about Wilder, written neatly on the strips of yellow paper he attached to his clipboard. He expected an apology; otherwise, he would resign. Wilder apologized. As the days passed, the arguments continued as surely as the apologies followed.

James Cain writes peerlessly stripped-down prose, but he lacks Chandler's descriptive vigor and, above all, his trenchant ways with dialogue. Wilder wanted to keep many of Cain's original exchanges, but Chandler felt they lost their effectiveness when spoken. They discussed the matter with Cain, who

FRED **MacMURRAY** ★ BARBARA **STANWYCK**
EDWARD G. ROBINSON

From the Moment they met it was Murder!

in PARAMOUNT'S

DOUBLE INDEMNITY

with
PORTER HALL
JEAN HEATHER
BYRON BARR
RICHARD GAINES
JOHN PHILLIBER
DIRECTED BY
BILLY WILDER
Screenplay by Billy Wilder and Raymond Chandler

Double Indemnity (1944): Chandler's first, and best, work for the cinema.

agreed that the speech passages were intended for the eye rather than the ear. "Chandler," Cain later remarked, "an older man a bit irked by Wilder's omniscience, had this odd little smile on his face as the talk went on."

While retaining Cain's fundamental narrative and motivation, Chandler and Wilder modified much of the peripheral detail. Walter Huff became first Walter Ness then—following the discovery of an insurance salesman of that name in Palos Verdes—Walter Neff. The Nirdlingers were transformed, without syllable loss, into the Dietrichsons. Nettie, the name of Huff's secretary, became the name of Phyllis Dietrichson's maid. Walter's bungalow in Los Feliz, where he has a Filipino houseboy, was changed to an apartment in the Wilshire area, where he makes do with a twice-weekly "colored woman"; Phyllis's house in Hollywoodland was moved to Los Feliz. The leisurely development of their association, involving numerous visits and considerable small talk, was compressed and accelerated. An elaborate subplot concerning Nino Zachetti, Phyllis's stepdaughter Lola's boyfriend, was dropped and his character toughened. At the book's conclusion, Neff meets Phyllis on a steamer to Balboa and they make a suicide pact by moonlight. To this, Chandler and Wilder gave a complete overhaul.

More significantly, they decided to develop the crucial relationship between Neff and the peevishly fastidious claims manager Keyes, and charged the early scenes between Neff and Phyllis with a predatory, erotic playfulness.

When the script was finished, Wilder looked for actors who would bring it to life. There was an immediate reluctance among Hollywood's leading men, who were required to display at least a measure of consistency in the kinds of roles they played. A likeable but corruptible hustler like Walter Neff who falls for an adulterous blonde and then kills her husband to get both the girl and the money seemed to fit no one's career plans. Even George Raft, not noted for his powers of discernment, is reputed to have turned it down. Neff, it seemed, spelled professional suicide.

It did not help matters that Wilder was disliked by Paramount's West Coast head of production, Y. Frank Freeman, a Baptist from Georgia whose chronic addiction to Coca-Cola was eclipsed only by his unswerving hatred of anyone he might consider to be a reprobate. Bob Hope and Bing Crosby, whose *Road* pictures were made at Paramount, had a running joke about him. "Y. Frank Freeman?" one would ask. "I don't know," the other would reply, "Y. Frank Freeman?"

Also working at Paramount was Fred MacMurray, who had been contracted to the studio for some years and had made his name as Claudette Colbert's leading man in *The Gilded Lily*. Since then he had been a lawyer, a rice planter, an aviator, a reporter, a Texas Ranger, and a Virginia cavalier. The idea of playing an all-American achiever with lust in his heart, money on his mind, and murder in his method was alien to the point of absurdity. His lack of interest was matched only by Billy Wilder's unyielding tenacity.

"After reading the script," MacMurray recalled, "I saw Billy at lunch and told him it was very good but I didn't want to do it, principally because I didn't know whether I could handle it. Up to that point, I'd done a lot of comedies and I was worried about what people would think. I was sure nobody would like it. The next day Billy asked me again, and the day after that. So I read it again and, despite a certain amount of opposition, I decided to take a crack at it and thank God I did because it's the best thing I've ever done. I know why Billy wanted me to do it. If he'd got Bogart or somebody like that, the audience would have known instantly that the couple was going to knock off the husband. With me in it, Neff was just a smart-alec who got hooked. It didn't require a great deal of acting. If a scene is well-written, as all of them were, you might just be standing there wondering when there would be a break for lunch. The audience plays a lot of those scenes for you."

For Phyllis Dietrichson, Wilder wanted Barbara Stanwyck, whom he taunted into accepting the part. "I always visualized murderesses as brunettes," she remarked while doing tests in blonde wigs, "but apparently blondes are considered harder and more unscrupulous, this season at least." When Edward G. Robinson agreed to play Keyes, the lead trio was complete.

Double Indemnity establishes its mood of somber desperation from the first frame. Behind the credits, a silhouetted figure on crutches advances toward camera, gradually filling the screen. A car travels fast along a dark, wet street in downtown Los Angeles early in the morning. A wounded man (MacMurray) walks into the offices of the Pacific All-Risk insurance company, greets the night porter, and goes to his desk, where, with some difficulty, he sits next to a record-

A smart-alec who got hooked: Barbara Stanwyck and Fred MacMurray in **Double Indemnity** (1944).

ing cylinder and dictates a confession in the form of a memo to the firm's claims manager, Barton Keyes. From this point on, Neff (MacMurray's character) continues his dictation intermittently and his narration—in a tradition that Chandler had already made his own—acts as the linking device of the film.

Some months earlier, Neff tells us, he had stopped at the Dietrichson family's Spanish Colonial Revival style house near Los Feliz Boulevard to encourage them to renew a car-insurance policy. Mr. Dietrichson is not at home but his wife emphatically is. Greeting him wearing only a towel, on account of some interrupted sunbathing, she stands at the top of the stairs while his bewitchment takes hold at the bottom. He waits in the living room as she dresses, the narration providing Chandler with the opportunity for some characteristically descriptive flourishes: "The living room was still stuffy from last night's cigars. The windows were closed and the sun shining in through the venetian blinds showed up the dust in the air. On the

"I wish you'd tell me what's engraved on that anklet." "Just my name." "As for instance."
"Phyllis": Fred MacMurray and Barbara Stanwyck.

piano in a couple of fancy frames were Mr. Dietrichson and his daughter Lola, his daughter by his first wife. They had a bowl of those little red goldfish on the table behind the big Davenport. But to tell you the truth, Keyes, I wasn't a whole lot interested in goldfish right then, nor in auto renewals, nor in Mr. Dietrichson and his daughter Lola. I was thinking about that dame upstairs and the way she had looked at me, and I wanted to see her again, close, without that silly staircase between us."

When the staircase is no longer between them and she is seated opposite him, it takes only a minute of playful sparring ("Neff is the name, isn't it?" "Yeah, two 'f's,' like in Philadelphia, if you know the story." "What story?" "*The Philadelphia Story*") before Neff is bouncing around the ring. Cain was never like this.

[38]

NEFF: I wish you'd tell me what's engraved on that
anklet.

PHYLLIS: Just my name.

NEFF: As for instance?

PHYLLIS: Phyllis.

NEFF: Phyllis. I think I like that.

PHYLLIS: But you're not sure.

NEFF: I'd have to drive it around the block a couple of
times.

PHYLLIS: Mr. Neff, why don't you drop by tomorrow
evening around 8.30? He'll be in then.

NEFF: Who?

PHYLLIS: My husband. You were anxious to talk to him,
weren't you?

NEFF: Yeah, I was. But I'm sort of getting over the idea.

PHYLLIS: There's a speed limit in this state, Mr. Neff,
forty-five miles per hour.

NEFF: How fast was I going, officer?

PHYLLIS: Around ninety.

NEFF: Suppose you get down off your motorcycle and
give me a ticket.

PHYLLIS: Suppose I let you off with a warning this time.

NEFF: Suppose it doesn't take.

PHYLLIS: Suppose I have to whack you over the knuckles.

NEFF: Suppose I burst out crying and put my head on
your shoulder.

PHYLLIS: Suppose you try putting it on my husband's
shoulder.

MacMurray is remarkable throughout the picture, but nowhere
more so than in these early scenes with Stanwyck. He moves with
the unshrinking assurance of a man accustomed to having his own
way; one who enjoys the potential for conflict inherent in his work
as much for the cerebral exercise as for the financial reward; one
likely to use an infatuation as a departure point for testing out a
theory about cheating on insurance claims. When Phyllis asks him
to return one afternoon, instead of keeping an earlier appointment
with her husband, his suspicions are semaphored by his confron-
tational manner:

PHYLLIS: Aren't you coming in?

NEFF: I'm considering it.

PHYLLIS: I hope you didn't mind my changing the
appointment. Last night wasn't so convenient.

NEFF: It's all right. I was working on my stamp collection
anyway.

PHYLLIS: I was just drinking some iced tea. Would you
like a glass?

NEFF: Unless you've got a bottle of beer that's not working.

PHYLLIS: There may be some. I never know what's in the
icebox. Nettie! Oh, about those renewals, Mr.
Neff. I talked to my husband about it.

NEFF: Oh, you did?

PHYLLIS: Yes, he'll renew with you, he told me so. As
a matter of fact, I thought he'd be here this
afternoon.

NEFF: But he's not.

PHYLLIS: No.

NEFF: (deadpan) That's terrible.

PHYLLIS: Nettie! Nettie! Oh I forgot, today's the maid's
day off.

NEFF: Never mind the beer, iced tea'll be fine.

PHYLLIS: Lemon, sugar?

NEFF: Fix it your way. As long as it's the maid's day off,
maybe there's something I can do for you . . .
like running the vacuum cleaner.

When she comes to the point, it becomes apparent to him that
her interest in accident insurance conceals nothing less conclusive
than a desire to liquidate her husband, and not only his business interests. Neff, shocked by the idea and unsettled by her nerve, goes
to a bowling alley at 3rd and Western (Chandler is as insistently specific here as in his novels) to lose himself in activity. Later, Phyllis
shows up at his apartment, disclaiming any of the malicious intentions he ascribes to her. In no time, Stanwyck's sweater begins to take
on its fetishistic status of the Forties, and sweet nothings are whis-
pered feverishly: "I'm crazy about you, baby." "I'm crazy about you,
Walter." "The perfume on your hair. What's the name of it?" "I don't
know. I bought it in Ensenada."

Oscillating between moist-eyed seductiveness and regretful sorrow as the besotted Neff begins to surrender, Phyllis tells him that she is Dietrichson's second wife, marrying him out of pity after the death of his first wife, whose nurse she was. Since then, she says, her life has been a misery. While she weeps, he broods. While she broods, he outlines the details of a plan that will mean the end of Mr. Dietrichson. They part company with mutual assurances that their dedication to the murder, the money, and each other will be "straight down the line," a phrase that, in the course of the film, will become an incantation.

The only problem Neff can foresee is in his office. Keyes is more than a claims manager. He is a finely tuned dishonesty detector. He can recite a litany of statistics on murders, suicides, and accidents. "Every month, hundreds of claims come to this desk," he informs a luckless truck driver from Inglewood who had foolishly lodged a false claim. "Some of them are phonies. And I know which ones. How do I know? Because my little man tells me. Every time one of these phonies comes along, it ties knots in my stomach." Neff understands him well: "You're so damned conscientious you're driving yourself crazy. You wouldn't even say today's Tuesday unless you looked at the calendar. Then you'd check to see if it was this year's or last year's calendar. Then you'd find out who'd printed the calendar and find out if it checked with the World Almanac Calendar."

Edward G. Robinson is extraordinary as Keyes, playing him as an irritable perfectionist, a hard-headed, soft-hearted, rapid-fire statistician who launches into outbursts about company inefficiency and insurance minutiae with such bilious enthusiasm that it is difficult to suppress a supportive cheer. Neff is the company's star salesman and Keyes treats him with crotchety affection.

Unintimidated, Neff calls on Dietrichson, signs him up for the car renewal, and, on the pretence of requiring his signature on a duplicate sheet, secures it on the dotted line of an accident insurance policy with a double-indemnity clause, for which the company pays twice the settlement if the insured party is killed while traveling by train. Neff and Phyllis begin to have planning meetings, compellingly staged in a supermarket reconstructed in the studio. As a model, Wilder and his art director, Hal Pereira, took Jerry's Market on Melrose Avenue, just around the corner from Paramount, reproducing its interior on a soundstage, where shelves were stocked with groceries valued at

Keyes is more than a claims manager. He is a finely tuned dishonesty detector.

"Of all the cases of suicide on record, there's not a single one of suicide by leaping from the rear end of a moving train": Richard Gaines, Fred MacMurray, and Edward G. Robinson.

one million ration points (the film, set in 1938, was made when World War II had engendered a different currency), all guarded by four round-the-clock studio policemen. Wilder avoided any shots of a meat counter as he would have been unable to fill it, such was its scarcity. (Pereira had already solved the business of designing the insurance-company offices by copying the interior of Paramount's New York headquarters.)

Back in the office, Keyes offers Neff a post as his assistant, which he declines. "I picked you for the job," declares Keyes ruefully, "not because I think you're so darned smart but because I thought you were a shade less dumb than the rest of them. I guess I was wrong. You're not smarter, Walter, you're just a little taller."

A telephone call from Phyllis warns Neff that Dietrichson, who has broken his leg, will be boarding a train that evening. In the film's most beautifully sustained sequence of scenes, Neff plants his alibis, changes into a suit resembling Dietrichson's, fakes a cast on his leg, and hides in the back of the Dietrichson car. At an agreed moment during the drive to the station, Neff reaches from behind and kills Dietrichson, which Wilder conveys with a single revealing close-up of Phyllis's face. On the observation platform of the train, from where Neff plans to jump off and "replace" himself on the railway line with the dead Dietrichson, he is joined by a man who, even under more convenient circumstances, populates nightmares— the hearty, garrulous fellow traveler. Neff dispatches him to fetch a cigar while he jumps from the train at the place where Phyllis has arranged to collect him in the car. Having deposited Dietrichson's body and crutches on the track, the couple prepare themselves for a getaway.

Where Cain restricts the suspense to their sudden realization that they have failed to plant a vital hat next to the body, Chandler and Wilder exploit the anxiety of the moment to within a whisper of the breaking point. Phyllis is unable to start the car. Agonizing seconds, resembling entire lifetimes, pass. The motor comes to life. The respiration regains its rhythm.

After the event, Neff's narration reaffirms his numbness: "I couldn't hear my own footsteps. It was the walk of a dead man." Keyes considers the claim, concluding that Dietrichson's death was an accident and that the company will have to pay. "Of all the cases of suicide on record," he declares, "there's not a single one of suicide by leaping from the rear end of a moving train." Norton, the head of the company, is unconvinced and has brought in "the widow" for cross-examining.

Barbara Stanwyck is at her most dazzling during this confrontation, which is also, tellingly, Phyllis Dietrichson's most important and impressive performance as a grieving woman. "Straight down the line," in the tradition of the litany she and Neff continue to exchange as a rallying code, she personifies the kind of murderer who would assess her appearance in mourning clothes *before* the event, as Lola will subsequently claim, and increase in resolution as lesser wills dissolve around her. When Norton proposes a compromise settlement, she strides out of his office with imperious conviction, projecting perfectly the injured pride of the newly bereaved. Neff, meanwhile, is developing the mannerisms of a guilty man. "I put on my glasses," his narration observes at one point, "so that people couldn't see my eyes. Then I took them off again so that they wouldn't wonder why I wore them."

The comfort of Keyes's support is short-lived. He arrives unannounced at Neff's apartment to express suspicions prompted by the fact that Dietrichson had an accident policy but failed to put in a claim

It was murder, his "little man" has decided and conveyed by giving him a fit of indigestion.

when he broke his leg. This means it was murder, his "little man" has decided and has conveyed by giving him a fit of indigestion. The stepdaughter, Lola, is as unsettled as she had once been when her mother died of pneumonia in front of an open window while under the care of Phyllis, her nurse. To provide a conciliatory smokescreen, while concurrently assuaging his conscience, Neff begins to spend considerable time with Lola: a Mexican dinner here, a spin in the car there, and before long the spring is back in his step.

Keyes develops a theory that duplicates the truth with unerring accuracy: "Murder is never perfect. It always falls apart sooner or later. When two people are involved, it's usually sooner. Now we know the Dietrichson dame is in it *and* the somebody else. Pretty soon, we'll know who that somebody else is. He'll show. He's got to show. Sometime, somewhere, they've got to meet. Their emotions are all kicked up. Whether it's love or hate, it doesn't matter. They can't keep away from each other. They may think it's twice as safe because there are two of them. But it isn't twice as safe. It's ten times twice as dangerous. They've committed a murder. And it's not like a trolley ride together where they can get off at different stops. They're stuck with each other and they've got to ride all the way to the end of the line and it's a one-way trip and the last stop is the cemetery." (Robinson's memory for the long speeches he had written for him delighted Chandler, who was a fully salaried regular presence on the set.)

Unnerved by Keyes's insight, Neff meets Jackson, the man from the observation car who has traveled down from Medford, Oregon, at Keyes's invitation and voices some pride in the integrity of its residents. "We're not in Medford now," Keyes informs him tetchily. "We're in a hurry." The bond between Neff and Phyllis is disintegrating in almost direct proportion to the increase in his affection for her stepdaughter. Sitting up in the hills behind the Hollywood Bowl, listening to Cesar Franck's D Minor Symphony—which composer Miklos Rozsa has punctuated effectively throughout the film—Lola announces her suspicions about an affair between Phyllis and Nino Zachetti.

Informed by Keyes that he has found a likely suspect in the case, Neff searches the office to discover his identity. He plays back a dictaphone memo from Keyes to Norton, affirming Neff's certain innocence and Zachetti's likely guilt. With such a scapegoat, all that remains is for him to get rid of the increasingly demanding Phyllis.

They arrange a rendezvous at her house. She is waiting for him when he arrives. They shoot each other in a scene of blackest poetry, the smell of honeysuckle sweetening the night air, the sound of the tune "Tangerine" mournfully drifting out of a neighbor's radio and filtering in through the shutters.

Back to the present: Neff is bleeding to death in Keyes's office. Keyes himself, alerted by the night porter, is behind him listening to the end of his confession. In an enfeebled attempt to escape, Neff staggers no farther than the elevator before collapsing. He fumbles for a final cigarette but is unable to light it, despite having struck a match (deftly, with his thumbnail) for Keyes's cigar throughout their friendship. Keyes, aware of the irony, reciprocates, watching over him sadly, a troubled father witnessing the last gasps of his wayward son.

Originally, the film ended with MacMurray taking his final breath in the gas chamber, but after spending $150,000 on building the set and five days on shooting the scene, Wilder developed doubts about its appropriateness and decided to substitute the existing ending.

Cheerless, abrasive, pessimistic, *Double Indemnity* is simply one of the best films of its kind ever made (just as the version made for television in 1973 with Richard Crenna and Samantha Eggar is one of the worst.) Like *Gilda, The Lady From Shanghai*, and Wilder's own *Sunset Boulevard*, it is narrated by a male central character adrift in a world where a woman calls the tune; where sex, money, and the inevitably of betrayal are constant companions; where shadows abound regardless of how many lights are turned on. Charles Higham and Joel Greenberg summarized it admirably: "*Double Indemnity*, one of the highest summits of *film noir*, is a film without the slightest trace of pity or love . . . As in *Mildred Pierce*, the Californian ambience is all-important: winding roads through the hills leading to tall stuccoed villas in a Spanish style thirty years out of date, cold tea drunk out of tall glasses on hot afternoons, dusty downtown streets, a huge and echoing insurance office, Chinese Checkers played on long pre-television evenings by people who hate each other's guts."

The critics of the period were equally enthusiastic, and even Alfred Hitchcock, never renowned for the plenitude of his praise, responded to Paramount's self-aggrandizing copyline—"The two most important words in pictures since *Broken Blossoms*"—by sending Wilder a telegram that read, "Since *Double Indemnity*, the two most important words are Billy Wilder."

The two endings: the one Wilder used . . .

. . . and the one he didn't.

Both the film and Chandler and Wilder's screenplay were nominated for Academy Awards, which they lost to Leo McCarey's *Going My Way*, Paramount's other contender and clearly the studio's own favorite. Wilder's biographer, Maurice Zolotow, tells the story of how Wilder, not a gracious loser when he sensed an injustice, tripped up McCarey as he walked to the stage to collect his award, leaving him in an undignified heap on the carpet.

Zolotow also quoted some of Chandler's subsequent *Atlantic Monthly* article to Wilder, and received a predictably explosive response: "Hollywood treated him badly? We didn't invite him to the preview? How could we? He was under the table drunk at Lucey's. It's a wonder they don't say Hollywood drove him to drink. Don't fall for that dreck—what Hollywood did to Raymond Chandler. What did Raymond Chandler do to Hollywood?"

A studio press release announcing the film assured its readers, "Unlike his detective, Chandler rarely touches alcohol at any time, and never while working. When at his work, Chandler stimulates himself continually, and exclusively, with tea." How his colleagues must have laughed. As well as keeping a bottle in the office to help him cope with Wilder, Chandler responded all too easily to the climate of genial dipsomania that prevailed in the writer's building and continued after work at Lucey's, the bar and restaurant across the street from Paramount.

More than twenty-four years later, on November 18, 1968, the State of California brought to trial a former insurance adjuster and the wife of a department-store stock clerk in Los Angeles. They were charged with murdering the woman's husband, trying to make it appear as if he had died in a fire, and collecting $35,000 on two insurance policies. The man was also charged with murdering his own bride of seven weeks, on whom he had taken out a double-indemnity policy worth $50,000.

The opening paragraph refers to *Double Indemnity,* the book and film that allegedly inspired the scheme. Real life, which had once provided James Cain with the material for his novel, was now considered merely imitative.

CHAPTER 4

TEARS AND TERROR

And Now Tomorrow, The Unseen

November 1943: Paramount executives were rolling out the red carpet for Corporal Alan Ladd, who had been given an honorable discharge following ten months service in the U.S. Army. Ladd was the studio's pre-eminent box-office star, and they were delighted to have him on the lot again, reinforcing his return with a massive publicity and advertising campaign to build anticipation for his "comeback" picture.

The screenplay of *Double Indemnity* was progressing sufficiently well to prompt Raymond Chandler's employers to seek maximum mileage from their new contract writer. He was assigned to assist Frank Partos, mainly on dialogue polish, in his adaptation of Rachel Field's *And Now Tomorrow,* a tear-drenched best-seller about how the haves and have-nots of a small mill town in New England learn to appreciate each other. Field, who had once worked as an editor in Paramount's story department for $45 a week, sold the studio her lachrymose blockbuster for $75,000 while Chandler had just disposed of *The Big Sleep* to Warner Bros. for his best fee yet—a modest $10,000.

The first role the production department had lined up for Ladd was that of Dr. Merek Vance, a young practitioner from the wrong side of the tracks whose newly developed serum restores the hearing of

Alan Ladd and
Loretta Young
sit on a
tear-drenched
best-seller:
**And Now
Tomorrow**
(1944).

a lofty local aristocrat, played by Loretta Young (who had already co-starred with Ladd in *China*). Susan Hayward and Barry Sullivan were given the roles of Young's sister and fiancé. Sullivan had appeared in *Lady in the Dark* with Ginger Rogers and *Rainbow Island* with Dorothy Lamour, but was otherwise fresh from Broadway.

"I had come from stage work in New York," he recalled, "and, like everyone from that background in those days, I had a very sophomoric attitude toward Hollywood. We were involved in an art form. Hollywood wasn't. My acting was absolutely god-awful. I was all over the screen, playing to the balcony, thinking that projection meant volume. Alan Ladd was the first person who ever taught me anything about film. He was simply the kindest, gentlest, most helpful person I've met in the business. Alan knew film technique well and was rarely given the credit he deserved as an actor—not even in *The Great Gatsby*, which I did with him a few years later.

"The director, Irving Pichel, was a pain in the ass. He refused to understand Alan's problem, which was his height. Pichel had a heavy-handed sense of humor and went out of his way to embarrass Alan. Sometimes he was brutally, vituperously insulting. I didn't get much direction, either. Theater actors from New York were almost revered (I don't know why, most of us stank), and the front office told directors not to bother directing people like myself, who didn't know a goddamn thing about motion pictures. I used to see Raymond Chandler on the set, behaving very much like an observer, and I only got to know him because we'd go across the street at lunchtime and have a couple of snorts at Lucey's. Later, I played Philip Marlowe in a radio adaptation of one of his books; but when you know somebody in the present, you never think they will eventually be legends. The subject matter of *And Now Tomorrow* certainly wasn't Chandler's style. It was just a soap opera. Maybe they put him with Frank Partos to learn something about screenwriting."

Chandler would not have agreed. He believed that he understood clearly the differences in technique between effective film and novel writing and was particularly conscious of both the potency and insufficiency of dialogue. Writing in 1951, he observed: "A preoccupation with words for their own sake is fatal to good filmmaking. It's not what films are for. The best scenes I ever wrote were practically monosyllabic. And the best short scene I ever wrote, by my judgement, was one in which a girl said 'uh huh' three times with different intonations, and that's all there was to it." (He is referring to *The Blue Dahlia,* released in 1946.)

Excepting two days on location at the Paramount Ranch in Calabasas—where art directors Hans Dreier and Hal Pereira created a typical New England village green complete with stores, trees, and war monument—the entire picture was shot in the studio. On one stage, Dreier and Pereira built the interior of the imposing Blair house, which impressed even Loretta Young, already developing some local fame as a decorator. *And Now Tomorrow,* it must be said, is the kind of film that would make any actress seek fame as a decorator.

An indefinitely postponed engagement: Barry Sullivan and Loretta Young in **And Now Tomorrow** (1944).

"That means you can't do anything for me," decides Emily Blair (Young) at the end of yet another consultation with a New York specialist who confirms that her deafness is beyond cure. On her way back to Blairstown, named after her family (which controls the local mill), she reminisces about her collapse from meningitis at a party celebrating her engagement to Jeff Stoddard (Sullivan). Waking up surrounded by people making noises she is unable to hear, she naturally concludes that she has gone deaf and suggests to Jeff that because of this, their engagement should be postponed indefinitely.

Changing trains at Boston while recovering from her reverie, she is rescued from certain death under the wheels of a luggage truck by Dr. Merek Vance (Ladd), who has already seen, and approved of, her reflection in the station coffee-bar mirror. She is frosty toward him but tolerates a taxi ride with him on arrival in Blairstown. "You read lips remarkably well," he enthuses before the chip on his shoulder regains its visibility. Vance is a poor boy of the town and has a grudge the size of a small continent against the Blair family because his father, a mill hand, was dismissed and demoralized into an early grave.

Meanwhile, Jeff has begun an affair with Emily's sister Janice (Hayward). Reluctant to reveal this to Emily, the lovers confine

themselves to sharing rather glum tea-times. His infatuation is un-
derstandable. Janice is a much better dancer than Emily, who, unable to hear the music, keeps stumbling, losing more in decorum
than she gains in pity.

Vance, who chain-smokes in his office, is anxious to help Emily
but will not tolerate any of her superior nonsense. Once, after she
fails to arrive on time for an appointment, he goes out to play pin-
ball, solely to keep her waiting and teach her a lesson. The most il-
luminating lesson of all, however, is one she teaches herself. During
a visit to the Blair house, Vance is called out urgently to attend a sick
child in Shantytown,
which enables Emily to experience the squalor she
has disregarded. Watching
and assisting Vance con-
duct a difficult operation,
she becomes aware of the
gulf between herself and
the boy's mother, with
whom she once attended
school. Past differences
forgotten over shared ex-
periences, she emerges a
new woman.

Vance, increasingly
charming, continues to
modify his serum, employ-
ing such trial subjects as
the auditory nerve of an
albino rabbit. Emily con-
tinues to look at people's
lips. Love, it becomes evident, means never having
to say you're deaf. Vance
makes final changes to the
serum and Emily becomes
its first recipient. At one
point, she is not only deaf
but nearly dead. When she

Vance (Alan Ladd) and Emily (Loretta Young) in his office. No
evidence of an albino rabbit.

Vance (Alan Ladd), a young practitioner from the wrong side of the tracks.

Love means never having to say you're deaf: Alan Ladd, Cecil Kellaway, and Loretta Young.

awakens, however, it is clear that the albino rabbit's auditory nerve has not been sacrificed in vain—she can hear the rain on the window and, quite content to encourage her fiancé and sister to consummate their guiltily suppressed lust, she rushes into the arms of the underprivileged genius who restored her hearing. As the final flourish of the score recedes, one can hear something else: the sound, perhaps subliminal, of a turkey gobbling.

Richard Winnington, writing in *News Chronicle*, viewed the film as more than a routine romantic melodrama, although he saw it was that as well: "The legend is that one of Poor Little Rich Girl v. Rich Little Poor Boy—compounded from the unfailing chemical formula that turns red litmus blue. And this is the point: it is much more subtly political, from the other side, than the banned *Potemkin* or *The Grapes of Wrath* . . . The form here is classic: Boy born in slums sees father exploited, sacked, and destroyed by mill-owning Blair family; Little Blair daughter becomes symbol of Boy's hatred; Boy grows up into brilliant young ear specialist; Girl, still haughtily grinding down poor, becomes incurably deaf through meningitis. What is more natural than for the doctor, still loathing her and her class, to treat and cure her with his new serum? What is more natural than that his slowly dawning worship of her courageous, beautiful, aristocratic soul should reach full flood when she delicately holds the torch during an emergency operation on a little slum boy? Thus the doctor, his resentment burned out in the magic flame of love, discovers (with us) that the Blair family is much finer and less jealous than the people they exploit. Blair blood is more than simple faith."

Time, treading warily on its customary political tightrope, restricted itself to unbridled sarcasm: "This sort of comedy of the inhumanly vindictive antagonism by which a man and a woman protract the ultimate inevitable plunge into each other's arms has, even at its silliest, some basis in truth. It is by no means new 1) to identify this skirmishing of the sexes with class warfare, 2) to resolve all class distinctions in the clinch. The only thing that gives this thousandth version any novelty is Alan Ladd's triple-chilled proficiency at handling all the tricks of making love in reverse gear. This is as interesting to look at, in a simple-minded way, as someone drinking a glass of beer standing on his head. But it probably takes a great deal more talent."

Bosley Crowther of the *New York Times* dismissed it as "a very stupid little movie" but reserved most of his bile for Loretta Young, whose performance he compared with "Fanny Brice's imitation of a glamorous movie queen. Whatever it was this actress never had, she still hasn't got." Only the trade publications—reluctant in those days to bite the hand that fed them—had anything remotely approving to say about it. This did not prevent a stampede to the box office.

If it is difficult to discern any trace of Chandler in *And Now Tomorrow,* it is practically impossible in *The Unseen,* the next rewrite that Paramount assigned to him. John Houseman, preparing for his first picture as a studio producer, was looking at material toward this end and chanced upon a minor-league English mystery story, *Her Heart in Her Throat* by Ethel Lina White—the writer of *The Wheel Spins,* from which *The Lady Vanishes* was adapted. A screenplay was commissioned from Hagar Wilde, who was recalled by Houseman as "a witty, neurotic lady, the author of many stories for women's magazines and one Broadway play; she had poodles, migraines, and marital problems and insisted on working at home. But she was a fast writer and within a few weeks she had done the first half of the script—the easy half."

The problem was to find a plausible conclusion to an implausibly serpentine plot. Wilde fell ill, so Houseman spoke to William Dozier, who supervised the studio's writers, and he came up with the idea of asking Chandler to complete the script, then rewrite whatever was necessary. It signalled the beginning of an association between Chandler and Houseman that was to continue for several years.

The director was Lewis Allen. Described by the *Los Angeles Times* (in a story that also refers to him as an eight-year-old) as "one of the most promising young megaphoners in the business," Allen had already made two movies for Paramount: *The Uninvited* and *Our Hearts Were Young and Gay.* Both starred Gail Russell, generally acknowledged to be "difficult" and, as one of the stars of the film in prospect, someone whom Allen already had experience of controlling. *The Uninvited* had been a success for Paramount, Allen, and producer Charles Brackett, whose first picture it had been following the dissolution of his partnership with Billy Wilder over *Double Indemnity.* It was an achievement the studio was anxious to repeat, so the film's

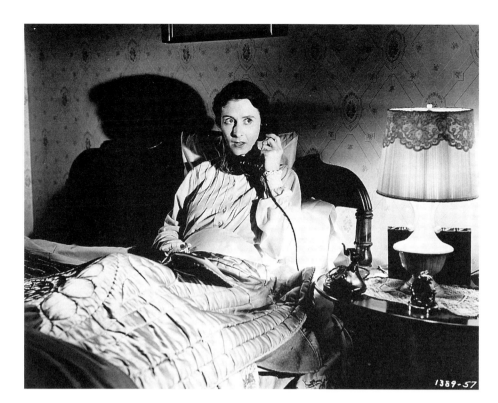

Bumps in the night in **The Unseen** (1945).

The son (Richard Lyon) and daughter (Nona Griffith) of the house.

The new governess,
Gail Russell.

The old governess,
Phyllis Brooks.

working title of *Fear* was changed first to the novel's (*Her Heart in Her Throat*) and finally—in an attempt to make the title as analogous as possible to *The Uninvited*—to *The Unseen*.

Allen had been Gilbert Miller's stage manager and eventual director in London and New York. Houseman disliked him enormously. "He had acquired from his master a veneer of theatrical expertise, bad manners, and snobbery," he wrote. "Flushed with his first directorial success on *The Uninvited*, he made no secret of his contempt for our script or of his disappointment at having to work with a nervous newcomer like myself after his recent association with the suave and prestigious Charles Brackett."

Allen, speaking before the publication of Houseman's memoirs, remembered Chandler as "very embittered. He felt he hadn't seen any decent money until he began working at Paramount. He did a complete rewrite on *The Unseen*. The English seem to handle terror better than Americans, and Ray—with his basically English attitude—understood what was needed. In fact, his main criticism of Hagar Wilde's script was that it was un-English, and he did his best to provide that. I don't think he ever really had the makings of a good screenwriter—his books were so descriptive, but in films the camera is the descriptive instrument. But he was a wonderfully down-to-earth guy who wouldn't stand for any nonsense, and he thought John Houseman was pompous. 'Look John,' he would say when Houseman tried to take his pencil to the script, '*I'm* the fuckin' writer!'"

Like *And Now Tomorrow, The Unseen* is set in a New England town invented on a drawing board and constructed in the studio, with one backlot exterior featuring the square where the sinister houses in which the action occurs are located. The story—so convoluted that one wonders if Chandler himself understood it—concerns various bumps in the night in a mansion that has been boarded up for the twelve years since its owner's death, and the house next door where Joel McCrea, embittered by the death of his wife under what he considers to be suspicious circumstances, is attempting to bring up a young son and daughter, whose presence on screen is frequently denoted by the frothily jaunty music one associates with the proximity of movie children. The son, played by Bebe Daniels' and Ben Lyon's son Richard, is huffy, abrasive, hypertense; the daughter (Nona Griffith) is cheerful, garrulous, eager to please. They are both, in their different ways, decidedly tiresome.

A doctor (Herbert Marshall, center) lives across the street and has a habit of materializing at moments of crisis.

Into this forbidding household wanders Gail Russell, the new governess ("You're pretty," someone observes forebodingly when she arrives. "Last one was pretty, too") who finds that the influence of her predecessor still has a grip on the children, particularly the boy. McCrea is none too cordial either, his range of reactions bounded by irritable terseness and sententious candor, which he switches between like windshield wipers in light drizzle. He is demanding on the nerves of the people around him, and in time becomes equally so on those of the audience. "That's where they belong," he tells Russell ominously after a low-angle shot of the children viewed through the upstairs bannister. "Behind bars."

A mysterious unidentified person murderously haunts the abandoned house next door, which a middle-aged woman arrives to claim.

The boy keeps the tap running to stay awake at night, leaves a toy elephant on the window sill and the downstairs door open, and receives payment from a secret employer. The girl has a newspaper picture of a corpse pasted in her scrapbook among the cut-outs of Snow White. Russell wanders around the house and cellar to investigate flickering lights and inexplicable sounds. A doctor friend of McCrea's (the reliably urbane Herbert Marshall) lives across the street and has a habit of materializing at moments of crisis.

This familiar cocktail of ingredients is shaken by John Seitz's shadowy lighting and menacing camera—as effective here as it was in *Double Indemnity*—and stirred by the exchanges between McCrea and Russell. Otherwise, it fails to deliver anything of lingering impact.

"I am forced to admit," conceded John Houseman, "that Allen shot the film as well as the material permitted and the surprisingly favorable reviews we received on its release were due in equal part to his direction, to the work that was done after the first preview by Chuck West (the studio's chief film editor), and to the personality and performance of our junior red herring." One of these reviews appeared in the *New York Herald Tribune,* which, praising the film with unwitting ambiguity, described it as "a mystery melodrama designed to give almost anyone the bona fide creeps." The doctor did it, by the way.

The largely routine work required of him on these films—and the concomitant loss of status they suggested following his Academy Award nomination—were among the likely contributing factors that prompted the backwash of bile contained in an article that Chandler wrote for *The Atlantic Monthly,* which appeared soon after the release of *The Unseen* in 1945.

Overstated in a manner implicit in polemical writing, the basic assertions are that producers, while occasionally quite tolerable as people (although he considers some to be "low-grade individuals"), wield excessive power; that directors are mostly hubristic, strutting idiots; and the writers, mediocre as many may be, never have the opportunity to become first-class citizens in the film process. "Hollywood," he felt, "seeks to exploit a talent without permitting it the right to be a talent . . . to me, the interesting thing about Hollywood writers of talent is not how few or how many there are, but how little of worth their talent is allowed to achieve . . . it is part of a deliberate and successful plan to reduce the professional screenwriter to the status of an assistant picture-maker, superficially deferred to (if he is in the room), essentially ignored, and even in his most brilliant achievements carefully pushed out of the way of any possible accolade that might otherwise fall to the star, the producer, the director."

As it would puncture his thesis, he does not acknowledge the positive elements of his life in Hollywood: the camaraderie he clearly felt with his colleagues, the respect with which he was treated, and the daily company of inquiring, amusing people. It was the first regular social contact he had enjoyed since beginning the solitary labor of writing.

"He loved to talk and argue about anything," observed screenwriter Robert Presnell to Chandler's biographer Frank MacShane, "and he usually dominated, though never with arrogance—but with an ironic humor. Studios were pretty easygoing places then, and writers were gentlemen of leisure. We'd take six or eight months to write a screenplay. There was a lady named Simone, who ran the Writers Building telephone switchboard, who always had coffee and snacks available (which we all paid for), and a fridge, where there was booze. If you wanted to start your day with champagne, you could. This is where we met each morning around ten o'clock, when we came to work. It was The Club, and Chandler presided. If the conversation got going well, some of us would spend the rest of the morning at it."

CHAPTER 5

MARLOWE SURFACES

Murder, My Sweet
(U.K. title: *Farewell, My Lovely*)

While Chandler led a relatively unproductive but extremely well-rewarded life at Paramount—one that afforded him the time and comfort in which to complain about it—history of a kind was being made next door.

Paramount's neighbor on Melrose Avenue was RKO—most of whose writers also drank at Lucey's—and Adrian Scott had recently become a producer there. Looking through the studio's story properties one day, much as John Houseman was doing farther down the block at Paramount, Scott decided that, as relatively few people had seen *The Falcon Takes Over* (RKO's rudimentary first attempt at filming *Farewell, My Lovely*), the story could be utilized again two years later without inviting attention; and as the studio paid no additional fee to the author for as long as it held the rights, at least one element in the budget would come cheaply. It would be, Scott declared, the first real attempt to transfer Chandler's lyrically sleazy universe to the screen, and with it that of his weary knight-errant, Philip Marlowe.

To write the script, he brought in John Paxton, with whom he had worked on the magazine *Stage* in New York. Paxton had not heard of Raymond Chandler at the time, but when he arrived the following morning, he read the book, watched *The Falcon Takes Over* (viewing it mostly as an indication of what to avoid) and began work on the screenplay, which he developed in close collaboration with Scott.

It was Scott's idea to use a first-person narration, acting as a counterpart to the novel and thereby retaining as much as possible of Chandler's language. "Once we decided on the narration," Paxton recalled, "there had to be a frame in which to tell it. We were serious young men of the theater, so although neither of us had any special regard for the plot, we didn't want to disregard the author's intentions. Most of the changes we made were to simplify the story, to tighten up unities of time and space, to make a strong, well-knit melodrama. I remember Adrian using the word 'intensification' a lot."

In the U.K. the title remained **Farewell, My Lovely** (1944) . . .

FORGET THAT FEELING...SHE'S GOT MURDER IN HER HEART!

An amazingly NEW Dick Powell—tough...rough...terrific!...Haunted by lovely face, hunted for another's crime...in a NEW kind of murder mystery!

Dick POWELL · Claire TREVOR · Anne SHIRLEY

Farewell My Lovely

OTTO KRUGER · MIKE MAZURKI · MILES MANDER · DOUGLAS WALTON · DON DOUGLAS

Produced by Adrian Scott · Directed by Edward Dmytryk · Screen Play by John Paxton

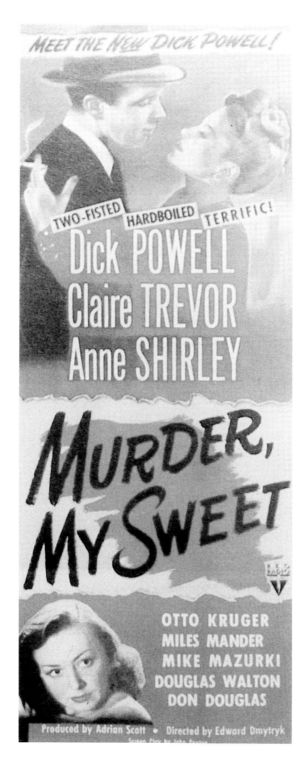

. . . while in the U.S. it became **Murder, My Sweet**.

An outsized simpleton looking for his Velma. Dick Powell as Marlowe, Mike Mazurki as Moose Malloy, and a man in the middle (who will not be there for long).

Marriott (Douglas Walton) calls on Marlowe, who is far from impressed with his calling card.

With this in mind, some of Chandler's narrative yielded to the pragmatic considerations of filmmaking; accordingly, characters, incidents, and locations were either eliminated or modified to fit requirements. Anne Riordan—the girl who finds Marlowe with a bump on the head and a corpse on his hands in a canyon near Malibu—is absorbed into the Grayle family, thereby excising one of the book's principal subplots in which her father, a former Bay City police chief, has been deposed by gambling racketeers led by a character called Laird Brunette, also removed in the transition.

Bay City is a thinly disguised Santa Monica, where Chandler lived on San Vicente Boulevard for a time in the late Thirties while writing the stories (*Try the Girl, Mandarin's Jade, The Man Who Liked Dogs*) from which the novel was, to use his own favored term, cannibalized. Bay City's principal characteristic, he felt, was its easy corruptibility, a condition facilitated by its small-town self-image and emphasized by local links between police, politicians, and the underworld. "The name's like a song," observes Marlowe at one point. "A song in a dirty bathtub."

"The Bay City police," explained Paxton, "confused the hell out of us. There were no moral, political, or philosophical considerations for getting rid of the parts that involved them. It wasn't an attempt to be nice to the police. It was an attempt to get a straighter storyline. We dropped Laird Brunette and his gambling ship from the plot for the same reason. Similarly, we wanted to develop the character of Moose Malloy and to make him more sympathetic, so he doesn't kill the owner of Florian's, nor did we make it an all-black bar as it is in the novel. These were just things we decided. Nobody outside the film saw the script until it was finished, so if there was any censorship, it was our own. We certainly knew we were treading on thin ice in some respects. A woman taking the sexual initiative, as Velma does with Marlowe, was virtually unheard of at the time."

Edward Dmytryk, the director of several B pictures for RKO—including, the year before, another Falcon film *The Falcon Strikes Back*—was assigned to direct. He, too, was concerned with retaining the Chandler essence. "Chandler is one of the very few novelists of any kind I know," he said, "whose dialogue you can recognize immediately." He also met him briefly and his recollection is of a lugubrious tippler: "He was rather a dour person and drank a good deal, as many people did and do in Hollywood, especially writers."

"Gardenias and playsuits do not go together": Claire Trevor, Miles Mander, Anne Shirley, and Dick Powell.

They had hoped to persuade John Garfield to play Marlowe. Garfield was then under contract to the studio, but many actors were going into the armed services and competition for people who had been declared unfit was considerable. Dick Powell had been classified 4F—in civilian terms, completely unacceptable—so RKO was anxious to lure him with the raw meat that a dramatic role would represent to a successful song-and-dance man in search of a challenge. It was common knowledge that Powell had coveted the part Fred MacMurray eventually played in *Double Indemnity* and had been disappointed at being dismissed as a pleasant tenor with aspirations. As RKO did not have the resources of other studios (they could not have afforded Bogart, for example), the script was the only inducement available for getting outside actors. Scott himself was perturbed by the prospect of casting a hoofer as the quintessential private eye, but Dmytryk was keen.

"I wanted Marlowe played," he related, "as I believed Chandler visualized him—really an Eagle Scout, a do-gooder, with the patina of toughness only skin deep. This good-guy characterization is implicit in many of the things Chandler had him say, and that is the way Powell played him. Not because that was what I wanted, but because that's what he was: an Arkansas farmboy who got into show business because his voice was too sweet for calling hogs, and who never quite got all the hay out of his hair."

Dmytryk attempted to develop Powell's confidence by involving him in all the technical aspects of the way a scene would be played. Eventually, Powell had heard enough. "Eddie," he said with exasperation, "just tell me what to do and I'll do it." "He was that kind of actor," Dmytryk reflected. "He certainly wasn't as good an actor as Bogie or Robert Montgomery or Bob Mitchum or even Jim Garner, and yet he was, I think, the best of the Marlowes."

In his book about screen detectives, William Iverson observed that Powell *became* Marlowe far more easily than, say, Bogart, around whom the lingering shadows of Sam Spade, Rick from *Casablanca*, and innumerable gangsters still gathered. Powell's Average Joe portrayal is certainly not as striking as Bogart's, nor as closely associated with him, but it remains enormously effective.

Farewell, My Lovely, as the film was at first called, begins with two outstanding scenes whose visual charge reinforces a mood of dispirited fatigue that has been violated by outsiders. The first is an overhead view of a table with a lamp, which casts a pool of light on Marlowe, gun-scorched, temporarily blinded, and bandaged around the eyes. Detectives in the shadows ask questions about why numerous corpses have materialized in his trail. He begins an explanatory narration. The second is in Marlowe's office, dark except for neon flickering from the street outside. When the light goes out, the window becomes a partial mirror reflecting the interior of the room, in which Marlowe observes a figure behind him. When the light returns, the image vanishes only to come back in the form of a towering outline, clearly that of a gigantic imbecile.

This is Moose Malloy (Mike Mazurki), who gives Marlowe forty dollars to accompany him to Florian's, a bar in downtown Los Angeles where his girlfriend, Velma, sang before Moose made an extended visit to the slammer eight years earlier. (This is the only film adaptation of the three that accords with the novel: five years of jail in *The Falcon Takes Over*, seven in the later *Farewell, My Lovely.*)

"Even on Central Avenue, not the quietest-dressed street in the world," wrote Chandler, navigating us toward one of his most celebrated similes, "he looked about as inconspicuous as a tarantula on a slice of angel food." Moose is as primitive as he is immense, and John Paxton deftly reinforces Chandler's turn of phrase with an epigram of his own: "I tried to picture him in love with somebody, but it didn't work."

As they walk along, Dmytryk further emphasizes Moose's height by persuading Dick Powell, in reality only a couple of inches shorter than Mazurki, to walk in the gutter while Mazurki takes the sidewalk. Once inside the bar, Velma's present whereabouts are politely but firmly requested. A flying body, having made the error of failing to cooperate with an obsessional giant, makes firewood of several tables and chairs. The bar's former owner, Jessie Florian, whom Marlowe later visits, delivers nothing more than a reluctantly proffered bogus photograph of Velma, an unattractive line in dressing gowns, and a propensity for guzzling other people's liquor.

The next figure in the maze is the twitchy Lindsay Marriott, played by Douglas Walton in a camel-hair overcoat across which we see the shadow of Marlowe's name on the office window. He offers Marlowe a hundred dollars to accompany him as he buys back a stolen jade necklace on behalf of a friend. Marlowe is open to offers of money because his income is such that he can hardly refuse them. One of the long-suffering policemen who pick up bodies after him is reproachful: "You're not a detective, you're a slot machine. You'd slit your own throat for six bits plus tax."

Marlowe's pragmatism, however, is matched by his ethical soundness. Offers of money for dropping a case are always refused, since he has usually accepted payment from someone else to continue the same investigation. When Marriott is murdered at the meeting place off Pacific Coast Highway after Marlowe has been struck a firm blow on the head ("A black pool opened up at my feet. I dived in. It had no bottom," a line of narration tranferred by Paxton from a later incident in the novel, provides the ideal prompting for Dmytryk's visual flourishes), he feels honor-bound to find his killer. "He gave me a hundred bucks to take care of him and I didn't," he declares. "I'm

"It's the sort of place where you have to wear a shirt": Claire Trevor and Dick Powell.

just a small businessman in a very messy business, but I like to follow through on a sale."

A girl he glimpses flashing a torch in his face as he regains consciousness turns up in his office the following day. She is Ann Grayle (for the film she undergoes the loss of an "e" on Anne, as well as a change of surname), and the stolen jade necklace belongs to her stepmother. It is difficult to speculate on what kind of stepmother Marlowe is accustomed to meeting, but it is unlikely that any of them looked like Claire Trevor. Having arrived at the Grayle mansion in Beverly Hills and done a little hopscotch on the hall floor's marble squares (a playful reminder of Powell's Busby Berkeley past, and his own idea), Marlowe strides into the drawing room and is introduced first to a superannuated jade collector, then to this wife, the archetypal Chandler temptress.

Blonde, carnal, manipulative, and learning to be at ease among the rich, she is impressively represented by Trevor. The *Hollywood Citizen News*, however, had several reservations about her clothing: "Claire Trevor's costumes reveal her to be a gal with a tawdry past, which she is trying to cover up with glitter and brilliance," it begins before obviousness gives way to pedantry. "In her first costume seen on the screen, which is a playsuit, she should be lolling on the beach. Instead, she is seen receiving guests in a stately drawing room. And she certainly should not be wearing a gardenia in her hair and at the top of her bra. Gardenias and playsuits," it concludes censoriously, "do not go together."

Indeed, she is a gal, to continue the newspaper's enviable vernacular, who is content to wear only a slip under her raincoat, as Marlowe will later discover. And she is a gal who is no stranger to the sight of a stranger's underwear. That evening, she visits Marlowe, gives him his third retainer of the film so far, and, catching sight of his torso barely restrained by a singlet, invites him to a nightclub. "It's the sort of place," she adds caustically, "where you have to wear a shirt." Once there, she disappears, leaving him to the attentions of Ann, who suggests further payment to abandon the case, and of Moose, who insists, in his quietly persuasive way, that he should meet someone.

The person in question is Jules Amthor—Otto Kruger with a carnation in his lapel—who lives in a splendid apartment in Sunset Towers from where, on a clear day, he claims in a single moment of lyricism, "you can see the ships in the bay in San Pedro." Marlowe, never at his most diplomatic among strangers, confronts him with the claim that Marriott was a blackmailer of rich, neurotic women and that Amthor pulled the strings.

Tactical soundness is not among Marlowe's principal assets. With this provocative piece of speculation, he has surrendered his few advantages. Amthor wants the necklace, which he assumes Marlowe has; Moose wants Velma, whom Amthor suggests Marlowe is hiding; and their combined brain and brawn leave him in a by now tiresomely familiar black pool. On this occasion, it is exacerbated by unfamiliar hallucinations: giant spectres of his aggressors; a series of doors that line up toward infinity; branches, syringes, whirlpools into which he tumbles inexorably; and, finally, the light on the ceiling as he awakes out of his eventual and protracted reverie. The problem is still far from over. "The window was open but the smoke didn't move," describes Paxton, skillfully contracting Chandler's account. "It was a grey web woven by a thousand spiders."

Simultaneously, the screen is fractured by a mosaic representing Marlowe's not entirely lucid frame of mind. "We tried several things," said Dmytryk, explaining how the effect was achieved. "What finally worked was that we photographed cigarette smoke, blew up the stills to huge proportions, and superimposed them, selecting a different frame for every shot so that I could have a fairly bare spot over a face I wanted to show. It tells you the whole story about his condition." David Selznick, who was producing *Spellbound* at the time and wrestling with the problem of its celebrated dream sequence, appar-

Marlowe up against Moose and Amthor (Otto Kruger, carnation, and gun).

ently consulted Dmytryk for advice. Preoccupied with his own film, Dmytryk was unable to give him any. In the end, Selznick's problem was resolved by hiring Salvador Dali.

Powell is remarkable in the scene: panicky, ravaged, debilitated by drugs, a character so alien to the condition in which he finds himself that he can never be quite sure when he is back on the rails again. "Now let's see you do something really tough," he admonishes himself in a direct quotation from the novel, "like putting your pants on." "Walk!" he keeps repeating in an attempt to make the spider's web disappear, only to find it returning inconveniently in the presence of the clinic's supervisor, Dr. Sondeborg, as he attempts to escape toward the comforting normality he craves. Leaving the location of his colorful and involuntary bender, his narration—"I wanted to go home and sleep a couple of hundred years"—coincides with the street sign Descanso. Descanso is Spanish for rest.

From then on, the opposing factions begin to converge. Marlowe, by now practically having peeled grapes placed in his mouth by an initially tetchy Ann, realizes who shone the torch in his face back in the canyon; Mr. Grayle is loading a gun and asking Marlowe to stop his investigation, which he has no intention of doing; Mrs. Grayle is at her seaside hideaway in Malibu, her presence revealed to Marlowe by a cloud of cigarette smoke hovering above the couch as he enters; Amthor has had his neck conclusively rearranged by an increasingly impatient Moose.

Separately, the survivors begin to gather at the beach house. Mrs. Grayle, far from pleased at being revealed as the villainous Velma, prepares to shoot Marlowe but is gunned down by her husband. Moose, who recognizes the blonde corpse in the raincoat as his beloved missing girlfriend, is also shot by Grayle, who, understandably, does not relish the prospect of Moose's wrath. (One of the most significant aspects of the novel's conclusion is that Moose is killed by the heartless bitch whom he has pursued reverentially like a giant poodle all the way through. Paxton says that he wrote several endings to the film before deciding on the existing one, which, he felt, "worked best in dramatic terms.")

The film cost $450,000 to produce and took forty-four days to complete. Chandler himself liked it very much and sent a complimentary note to Paxton saying so. It is certainly considered by many to be the most consistently enjoyable and imaginative Marlowe movie, and second only to *The Maltese Falcon* as the influencial detective thriller of the period. The *Los Angeles Examiner* thought it "the best murder melodrama since *Double Indemnity*."

The *New York Herald Tribune* called it "top-notch thriller fare." *Newsweek* thought it "a gaudy tale but a neat one." And Dilys Powell, who had already begun to champion Chandler's work in the London *Sunday Times*, wrote that it was "a brilliantly hard and fast film . . . Mr. Powell must now join Humphrey Bogart in a minute class of film actors who, looking at a woman, display something more than the enthusiasm of a clubman choosing a boiled shirt." Among the main critics, Manny Ferber in the *New Republic* was one of the few who remained unconvinced: "By all odds, the most incomprehensible film in years. The mystery gets solved just the same, by killing off everybody but the detective, his sweetheart, and the people who grill him in the first scene."

Dmytryk viewed it as one of those films that are continuously re-appraised: "It did quite well at the box-office, but *Life* magazine, for example, dismissed it when it first came out. Later on at the end of the year, they had a section for mistaken assessments they admitted to having made, and that was one of them. But in those days, none of us made films with the intention of them being regarded as classics. We simply never thought about it. I was lecturing at a school after I stopped directing and the students asked me to tell them about *film noir*. I asked them what *film noir* was and they told me I had helped to invent it."

Film Noir—fundamentally, a collision of pulp fiction, expressionistic lighting, and Sigmund Freud—is a term that inspires many film commentators to stray into giddy realms of theorizing precisely because its amalgam of elements is sufficiently abstract to allow one to impose it on virtually any shadowy, pessimistic, monochrome thriller of the period (or on those contemporary films that pay tribute to the genre.) A highly evocative, if elemental, summary of its constituents was provided by Charles Higham and Joel Greenberg: "A dark street in the early morning hours, splashed with a sudden downpour. Lamps form haloes in the murk. In a walk-up, filled with the intermittent flashing of a neon sign from across the street, a man is waiting to murder or be murdered . . . Standard lamps fall on pile carpets, spilling a fan of light about the face of a corpse; interrogation rooms filled with nervous policemen, the witness framed at their center under a spotlight; heels clicking along subway or elevated platforms at midnight; cars spanking along canyon roads, with anguished faces beyond the rain-splashed windscreen . . . here is a world where it is always night, always foggy or wet, filled with gunshots and sobs, where men wear turned-down brims on their hats and women loom in fur coats, guns thrust deep into pockets."

Another *film noir* trait is that its principal characters are often pursued by spectres of the past manifested through people of the present. In 1947, after completing his most radical film, *Crossfire* (like this picture, scripted by John Paxton and produced by Adrian Scott), Dmytryk, together with the nine others collectively referred to as the Hollywood Ten (Alvah Bessie, Herbert Biberman, Lester Cole, Ring Lardner Jr., John Howard Lawson, Albert Maltz, Sam Ornitz, Dalton Trumbo, and Scott himself), refused to tell the House Committee on Un-American Activities whether or not he was or had been a member of the Communist Party. He moved to London, where he made several films. On his return in 1950, he was convicted of contempt of Congress, fined, and sent to prison for six months. After serving his sentence, he recanted and returned to making movies, which he did always with competence if rarely again with brilliance until 1975, when he retired and turned to teaching. There has probably not been a single day in the past forty-five years that Dmytryk has not been asked a question about the Hollywood Ten.

As for the film under consideration, it was produced, previewed, and even opened under the title *Farewell, My Lovely*. Two days after it was premiered in Minneapolis, Audience Research Inc., a Gallup offshoot, persuaded its client, RKO, to change the title. The old title, they had decided, was unattractive to lovers of detective thrillers and confusing to those who might equate Powell's presence with a musical. The new, informative, alluring title was *Murder, My Sweet*.

CHAPTER 6

BOTTOM OF THE BOTTLE

The Blue Dahlia

Raymond Chandler's contract with Paramount expired in September 1944. Cushioned by having saved much of his substantial salary, supplemented by a share of the $10,000 that Warner Bros. had paid for the film rights to *The Big Sleep*, he returned to his house on Drexel Avenue and re-acquainted himself with the consoling presence of his wife and the cumbersome discipline of writing alone.

While his agent, H.N. Swanson, was negotiating new terms in the customary manner, Paramount executives found themselves facing the prospect of a disaster. The studio's golden boy, Alan Ladd, still the top star on the lot after a year out of uniform, was due to return to the Army three months later without a single film ready for release. At the next producers' meeting, the order was spelled out in flashing neon-lit capitals: find a project for Ladd and make it immediately.

John Houseman was among the producers on whose speed and acumen the studio was relying. He had remained friends with Chandler following their brief association on *The Unseen* and still met him for lunch occasionally or went for rides in Chandler's bungalow-sized Packard convertible. Their bond, Houseman reflected, was rooted in

Alan Ladd examining a blue dahlia for the benefit of a stills cameraman.
There is no such moment in the film.

Chandler's idea of Houseman as the only person at the studio other than himself who had been educated at a British public school and who, therefore, shared a code of conduct their Californian colleagues could never aspire to duplicate: "I think he hoped to recapture, in my company, some of the sounds and memories of his English childhood . . . And the English public school system had left its sexually devastating mark upon him. The presence of young women—secretaries and extras around the lot—disturbed and excited him. His voice was normally muted; it was in a husky whisper that he uttered those prurient juvenile obscenities at which he would have been the first to take offense if they had been spoken by others."

After the meeting, the studio telephones already monopolized by sounds of gravity and urgency, Houseman joined Chandler for one of the occasional old-school-tie lunches, which Chandler cherished as civilized encounters between like-minded people. In the course of it, Chandler lamented his inability to finish a novel he was writing, adding that he was considering turning it into a screenplay.

Two days later he was back at Paramount with a new contract, a salary of a $1000 a week, and a generous payment for his greatly appreciated Alan Ladd vehicle. Houseman was to produce it, with Joseph Sistrom—still respected by Chandler after their association on *Double Indemnity*—as executive producer. Within a fortnight, Chandler had written a letter claiming that "in less than two weeks I wrote an original story of ninety pages. All dictated and never looked at until finished. I begin to realize the great number of stories that are lost by us rather meticulous boys simply because we permit our minds to freeze on the faults rather than let them work for a while without the critical overseer sniping at everything that is not perfect."

He was working at a feverish pace, but then so was everybody else. While he delivered the first half of the script, the casting was concluded, together with as much of a shooting schedule as could be determined at this stage.

The actors presented no serious problems, Veronica Lake had already made three films with Ladd—*This Gun for Hire, The Glass Key,* and *Star Spangled Rhythm* (all 1942)—and was one of his favorite leading ladies. The principal reason for this is that she was short, thereby eliminating the need for any of the ego-assuaging use of orange boxes or digging of trenches that Ladd's sensitivity about his height led him to demand. William Bendix, a friend and frequent co-star in character parts, was not a threat either, but Ladd's considerable reservations about the statuesque Doris Dowling, who was to play his erring minx of a wife, were withdrawn only after he had been assured that she would be sitting or lying down during most of their big scene together.

The schedule was a matter dictated almost entirely by the daunting proximity of Ladd's call-up. At the helm was the veteran George Marshall, a director since 1917, and a man who understood that shooting on such a film, once begun, must adhere slavishly to plan. He had not also been an actor, prop-boy, make-up man, editor, cameraman, writer, assistant director, and studio executive for nothing. After three weeks of filming they were ahead of schedule; smiles of relief illuminated the soundstages. A few days later, Marshall began to gain on the script. With thirty pages still to be delivered, an obstacle guaranteed to perforate ulcers in the front office made itself apparent: Ladd's deadline was semaphoring from the horizon and Chandler had developed writer's block. More specifically, he had no ending.

The story so far was that Alan Ladd as Johnny has returned from naval flying heroics in the South Pacific with two maritime cronies, one of whom, Buzz (William Bendix), has a metal plate in his head as a result of a war wound. Consequently, he suffers from lapses of

Heroes back from the South Pacific: William Bendix, Hugh Beaumont, and Alan Ladd line them up in **The Blue Dahlia** (1946).

"That monkey music!"

memory, an unreliable temper, and an allergic reaction to real or imagined blasts of bebop, which he refers to with near homicidal antipathy as "that monkey music!"

Visiting his wife in her recently acquired hotel bungalow, Johnny finds her (Doris Dowling, not yet sitting but doing more stooping and leaning back than is advisable) none too sober and giving a rowdy party at which he has clearly not been expected. Among those present is Eddie Harwood (the impeccable Howard Da Silva), who owns a nightclub called The Blue Dahlia and has been dallying with Johnny's wife in his absence. Johnny, understandably unamused, breaks up the gathering and learns, during the subsequent quarrel with his now dutifully reclining wife, that their son's death was caused not by diphtheria, as he had been informed, but by her drunken driving. Their confrontation is remarked upon by the hotel detective, a creepy old blackmailer given to loitering around the grounds.

Buzz, told of Johnny's departure and going through a bad spell with the metal plate and the monkey music, decides to pay the wife an unannounced visit. Meeting him in a bar, she is as unaware of his identity as he is of hers. Meanwhile, equally ignorant of their link are Johnny and fellow ship-in-the-night Joyce Harwood (Veronica Lake), the estranged wife of his wife's lover, who picks him up in her car as he walks along in the rain and gives him a ride to Pacific Coast Highway.

Back in the bungalow, Johnny's wife is dead, shot by the revolver he had earlier been tempted to use but had instead tossed on a chair beside a discarded blue dahlia promoting Harwood's nightclub. So who fired the bullet? Was it Harwood, who visited her later that evening in response to a possible blackmail attempt? The house peeper, who was hiding behind a bush when Harwood left? Buzz, who tended at moments of stress to forget having done certain things?

This was at least part of the puzzle, as much of the remaining narrative had been completed. Joyce's discovery of Johnny's problem and her attempt to help him; his discovery of hers and his attempt to forget

Dead wife (Doris Dowling) discovered by maid.

her; the police questioning everyone they can find; numerous blackmail attempts; Johnny's discovery that Harwood is wanted for murder in New Jersey; Harwood's decision to have him kidnapped, and its consequences. But still no ending. Manicured nails drummed on table tops. Concern was rapidly giving way to panic.

Most concerned of all, understandably, was Raymond Chandler, who was the reason for everyone else's concern. One morning, Paramount's head of production called him in for a confidential meeting and outlined the studio's predicament. They were in trouble, he explained, or they would be very soon if Chandler's script were not completed on time. If he succeeded in doing so, they would show their appreciation with a bonus check for $5000.

Instead of providing the desired incentive and encouragement, the offer, said Houseman, succeeded instead "in disturbing Ray in three distinct and separate ways: One—his faith in himself was destroyed. By never letting Ray share my apprehensions, I had convinced him of my confidence in his ability to finish the script on time. This sense of security was now hopelessly shattered. Two—he had been insulted. To be offered an additional sum of money for the completion of an assignment for which he had already been contracted and that he had every intention of fulfilling was by Ray's standards a degradation and a dishonor. Three—he had been invited to betray a friend and fellow public-school man. The way the interview had been conducted ('behind your back, John') filled Ray with humiliation and rage."

He was, he insisted, incapable of further work on *The Blue Dahlia*; he had been thrown off balance, his reservoir had dried up, he was going home. The following morning he re-appeared in Houseman's office, where they silently weighed up the consequence of Chandler's decision. There was one other possibility, decided Chandler after a long interval. Not wishing to place Houseman in an awkward position, something people of their background were honor-bound to eschew, he might be able to complete the screenplay if he were to remain drunk throughout the process. He had abstained completely in recent months and, although writing well, he missed the consistent boost of confidence that alcohol invariably instilled in him.

Furthermore, he added, he had written out a list of requirements that, if agreed to, would minimize the health hazards that might otherwise afflict a man of his age and general debility. The studio was to provide two Cadillac limousines—constantly on call outside Chandler's house—to fetch the doctor, take the script to the studio, drive the maid to the supermarket, and anything else that might arise. Six secretaries, in relays of two, were to be available at all hours for dictation and typing. Nurses to administer vitamin shots were also required as Chandler never ate when on a bender. Finally, he wanted a permanently open telephone line to the studio.

Houseman took the memorandum for a ruminative ramble around the Paramount lot and finished up in Sistrom's office. Discussing the matter further, they reached the conclusion that, if this was the only way the film was going to be completed, they would accept the risk and make up a story to satisfy the studio potentates. Houseman returned to give Chandler the verdict: "With all the public-school fervor and esprit de corps that I could dredge up from the memory of my ten years at Clifton, I accepted the proposal."

To celebrate, they drove to a restaurant where Chandler stoked up his metabolism toward its intended level with three double martinis before lunch and three stingers afterward. When they returned to Chandler's house, the first squadron of limousines and secretaries was already in position, awaiting starter's orders.

For the next week, Chandler remained very systematically and quite productively pickled. There was nothing demonstrative about his perpetual drunkenness, no cries for more bourbon to illusory barmen, no stumbling around in some soused delirium. Having consumed the initial quantity, he simply kept himself topped up. When he fell asleep, as he did from time to time, he would awake later, picking up his drink and the end of the last sentence as if living in a continuum. It was, in many respects, just an exercise in getting something done.

The film was finished on time, Ladd went back into uniform, and Paramount, in the end delighted just to *have* the movie, grossed $2.75 million. It took Chandler a full month to recover, although some believe he never did. "When I came to see him," Houseman remembered, "he would extend a white and trembling hand and acknowledge my expressions of gratitude with the modest smile of a gravely wounded hero who has shown courage far beyond the call of duty."

Characteristically Chandler, despite a second Academy Award nomination, could find little merit in the outcome of his efforts. He had already been upset by what he considered to be the studio's acquiescent attitude to pressure from the U.S. Navy. Concerned about the way its heroes were reflected in popular entertainment, the Navy Department in Washington objected to Buzz being portrayed as a

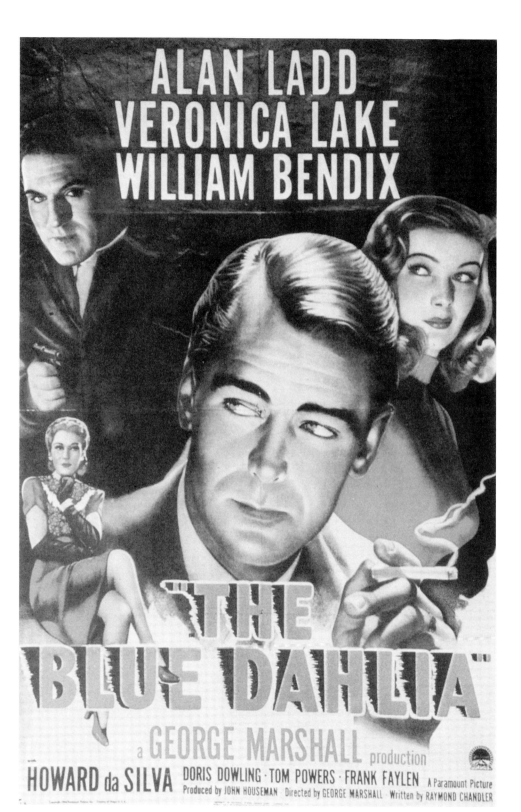

killer (Chandler's original intention) and persuaded Paramount to revise the ending.

"What the Navy Department did to the story," wrote Chandler to the critic James Sandoe, "was a little thing like making me change the murderer and hence making a routine whodunit out of a fairly original idea. What I wrote was a story of a man who killed (executed would be a better word) his pal's wife under the stress of a great and legitimate anger, then blanked out and forgot all about it; then with perfect honesty did his best to help the pal get out of a jam, then found himself in a set of circumstances that brought about partial recall. The poor guy remembered enough to make it clear who the murderer was to others, but never realized it himself."

The conclusion that replaced it was feeble by any standards. By Chandler's, it was almost risible in its banality. As the investigative finger begins to point at the hotel detective (who at one stage or another has attempted to blackmail practically everyone in the plot), he splutters

Veronica Lake was one of Ladd's favorite leading ladies. The main reason for this is that she was short.

out a spiteful little speech, makes a half-hearted attempt to escape, and gets shot. Partial curtain followed by modified epilogue: Chandler's script has Joyce driving off, leaving Johnny to tie one on with his buddies and adding the concluding line ("Did somebody say something about a glass of bourbon?") as a private joke about his liver-ravaging final week of writing. George Marshall changed it so that Johnny stayed with Joyce, leaving his pals to do their own drinking.

In fact, Marshall changed several things, only one of which—Don Costello, the actor playing Harwood's sidekick Leo, broke his toe so his injury was incorporated into the action—was purely circumstantial. Chandler was upset by these, but whether he threatened to "walk off" the picture unless Marshall stopped interfering with his dialogue, as he claimed, is debatable when one considers that much of the time he was barely capable of crawling out of his own study.

Indeed, Marshall, who remained silent on the subject for seventeen years, eventually found the propagation of this fable as fact too irksome to restrain himself any longer. In 1962, writing to the *Los Angeles Times* in response to a recent article, he praised Chandler but deflated the legend: "He was in no shape to walk anywhere—certainly not from the studio because he wasn't there and certainly not from home because at the time John Houseman, the producer, was either sitting on him or locking him in the closet to try to get the script finished."

Chandler was even more disparaging about "Miss Moronica Lake," as he rather boorishly called her in another letter to Sandoe about the film. "The only times she's good," he wrote with escalating bile, "is when she keeps her mouth shut and looks mysterious. The moment she tries to behave as if she had a brain she falls flat on her face. The scenes we had to cut out because she loused them up! And there are three godawful close shots of her looking perturbed that make me want to throw my lunch over the fence." Charming.

Veronica Lake was an obvious target for Chandler's disapproval since the nature of her success contravened all his ideas about achievement through talent and tenacity. As far as he was concerned, she had sold her hair. *Life* magazine's issue of November 24, 1941, even had a three-page spread devoted to an in-depth analysis of it. There were approximately 150,000 hairs on Miss Lake's head, it revealed, each about .0024 inches in width. She was obliged to arrive early each morning at the studio so that it could be washed twice in Nulava shampoo, once in Maro oil, and then rinsed in vinegar. She had to be careful not to catch it in elevator doors, electric fans, necklaces, or bracelets, and avoid singeing it while smoking. Paramount's promotion department was expected to invent a new name for her hairstyle every month, and unexpected support came from the U.S. government when women began to work in munitions plants. Many of them had Lake hairdos, making them, in the opinion of the authorities, not only half blind but a danger to themselves. In March 1943, the War Production Board began an advertising campaign, using photos of Veronica Lake, warning about the perils of hair getting caught in machinery.

Lake's performance in *The Blue Dahlia*, notwithstanding its limited scope, is a good deal more effective than Chandler's pronouncement would suggest. Indeed, her scenes with Ladd have an easy nonchalance that is as attractive to the viewer as it eventually becomes to them. In a screenplay that generally lacks the wit and imagination that Billy Wilder provoked out of Chandler for *Double Indemnity*, Ladd and Lake get the pick of the smart dialogue ("Practically all the people I know were strangers when I met them." "The man who killed her isn't going to get away with it; he just thinks he is.") Leo has a good line, too, well before he breaks his toe: "Just don't get too complicated, Eddie," he advises Harwood. "When a guy gets too complicated, he's unhappy. And when he's unhappy, his luck runs out."

Chandler's was just about to do so, despite the film's substantial box-office returns and favorable notices. The *Hollywood Reporter*, attempting to pack as many of its clichés as possible into the same

Tom Powers and a note-taking colleague interview Veronica Lake. This was Powers' second Chandler script in two years. He played Dietrichson in **Double Indemnity**.

appraisal, said that "the vehicle pulls no punches and with the name draw of its top-grade cast should be a sock at the box office. There is swell material for showmanly exploitation in this offering." The more restrained *Tribune* called it "a model of adroit filmmaking." Even the Daughters of the American Revolution, then a powerful opinion body of moralistic harridans, gave it their approval: "an exciting, intelligently handled, fast-moving murder film," said their preview committee. Paramount, for their part, did everything possible to emphasize Chandler's involvement: a prominent credit, a dinner in his honor at Lucey's, and a special screening to which most of the prominent mystery writers were invited.

In the summer of 1945—between the film's completion and its eventual release—Chandler went to MGM for three months to work on an adaptation of his fourth and most recent novel, *The Lady in the Lake*, with the by then inevitably acrimonious results. Taking a holiday while his agent discussed new terms with Paramount, and feeling he had earned the right to call the tune, Chandler rejected all their proposals and, on his return to Los Angeles, refused to turn up for work. Placed under suspension, he lamented his circumstances to Alfred Knopf, his publisher at the time: "One of the troubles is that it seems quite impossible to convince anyone that a man would turn his back on a whopping salary—whopping by the standards of normal living—for any reason but a tactical maneuver through which he hopes to acquire a still more whopping salary. What I want is something quite different: a freedom from datelines and unnatural pressures, and a right to find and work with those few people in Hollywood whose purpose is to make the best pictures possible within the limitations of a popular art, not merely to repeat the old vulgar formula."

His belief that hardly anyone in the movie business had integrity became a self-fulfilling prophecy, and he rarely encountered those who did. By the late spring of 1946, he had made his peace with Paramount and began work, with the mandatory collaborator, on an adaptation of Elizabeth Sanxay Holding's novel *The Innocent Mrs. Duff*, but after the agreed term he left again, with the screenplay unfinished and the customary complaints about interfering producers.

Weary of his defiance and disapproval, the studio's patience was wearing thin. When he left Hollywood and moved to a house by the sea in La Jolla, nobody cried.

When it was reissued, **The Big Sleep** (1946) had mysteriously become "the violence-screen's all-time rocker-shocker."

CHAPTER 7

SUGAR WON'T WORK

The Big Sleep

The original film version of Raymond Chandler's first novel was directed by Howard Hawks, who was infatuated with Lauren Bacall, and starred Bacall and Humphrey Bogart, who were infatuated with each other. Indeed, by the time shooting began on October 10, 1944, the romance was firmly under way, frustrated only by Bogart's reluctance to leave his demonstrative, dipsomaniacal wife, Mayo, and by Hawks' manifest disapproval of their association.

Bogart was forty-five, Bacall twenty. He drank like a dehydrated legionnaire, she touched nothing more intoxicating than fruit juice. They had met on the set of *To Have and Have Not* the previous year, he the marriage-scarred movie veteran, she the nervous newcomer, recently arrived in Hollywood, groomed by Hawks, and written into the picture at his instruction. As filming progressed, Bacall and Bogart had become inseparable, with Hawks brooding on the periphery, watching the girl in whom he had invested considerable time, money, imagination, and guidance—in effect, whom he had "created"—thirst for someone else.

Bogart and Bacall's screen partnership was as consummate a success as their personal association was to become, and Hawks, despite his silent but escalating displeasure, was anxious to take it a stage further with *The Big Sleep.*

As Chandler himself was unavailable to write the script because of commitments at Paramount, Hawks called in William Faulkner, co-writer of the screenplay of *To Have and Have Not* and an old friend. Hawks had first encountered Faulkner's work while making *Scarface* in New York in 1932, when, impressed by the novel *Soldier's Pay,* he had resolved to follow its author's progress. Soon after, he read Faulkner's *Saturday Evening Post* short story "Turn About" and suggested that he adapt it for the cinema, which he did in what eventually became *Today We Live* (1933). From then on, Faulkner worked on numerous films, several of them uncredited, many of them unproduced.

To Hollywood, Faulkner represented the prestige writer, professional enough to be flexible and respected enough to be useful. To Faulkner, Hollywood provided a means of remaining solvent. He was neither broken by it like F. Scott Fitzgerald, nor resentful of it like Chandler; he accepted it pragmatically as an expedient work location or, as he later described it to a friend, "a kind of purgatory, a place where it was necessary to come from time to time to do penance." Bacall thought highly of him. "He was a unique talent and a really interesting man," she said. "He took jobs when he needed the money, and he certainly wasn't worried about having to adapt somebody else's novel. He knew what was required without having to adjust his style to that of a 'Hollywood writer.'"

Throughout his time of working in the movies, Faulkner remained the fundamental outsider, a status confirmed by the apocryphal but characteristic story by which his years in Hollywood are always best remembered. One day he asked the studio people if he could work at home. They agreed, a little reluctantly as they preferred to have writers on the premises in case of emergency. Attempting to contact him on one such occasion, they did find him working at home—in Oxford, Mississippi.

His curiosity as a reader undiminished, Hawks came across a mystery novel called *No Good From a Corpse* by somebody called Leigh Brackett, whom he thought might be an appropriate collaborator for Faulkner on an adaptation as specialized as *The Big Sleep.* He telephoned the agent to inquire after Mr. Brackett's availability and was informed that it was a *Miss* Brackett who would come to see him.

She arrived at Hawks' bungalow at Warners the following morning and was greeted by Faulkner, immaculately dressed in tweeds and holding a copy of the novel. It would be best, he had already decided, if they were to work on alternate chapters, which he had marked accordingly. They went to separate offices and began writing, rarely consulting and never seeing each other's work. Hawks did not encourage collaboration in the Hollywood sense. As all the script was passed on to him for approval and revision, he was quite content for the writers to remain apart.

Between them, Faulkner and Brackett finished the first draft of the screenplay in eight days. "Writing the script of *The Big Sleep* presented me with very few problems," observed Brackett in an article for *Take One* magazine. "The book was good, and it was contemporary; the war was on, but even so, the idiom of 1939 was not far behind us. We were still living it, still speaking the same language. We updated the book in a few minor ways, such as the references to red stamps. Considering the rushing about done by Marlowe in his car, gasoline rationing and all, I don't think we even took that too seriously. Most importantly, though we didn't think about it then, the concept of the private eye—the tough, incorruptible, good-bad man who worked for justice by his own hard, unsentimental light—was still fresh and exciting. Along with Marlowe, we had the wealthy old man Sternwood, the beautiful and oversexed daughters, the handsome no-good gambler, the sympathetic hood, a sufficiency of unsympathetic ones, sexy ladies, solid brutality, high life in low places, and suspense all along the way. How could we lose?"

Despite having to carry the weight of Chandler's most serpentine plot, *The Big Sleep* is a lively, engaging departure point for a film adaptation, full of the vigor and vitality that alcohol, fatigue, and self-pity would later enervate. He had written it in three months in 1938—his first novel at the age of fifty—with publication the following year. Like *Farewell, My Lovely* and *The Lady in the Lake*, it plunders his own short stories, notably *Killer in the Rain* and *The Curtain*, and freely amalgamates characters.

When Faulkner and Brackett began writing the screenplay, they were already familiar with most of the changes that Hawks required, beginning with the placing of greater stress on the association between Marlowe and General Sternwood's elder daughter, Vivian, played by Bacall. "Howard enjoyed the way our personalities played

636-1

"She tried to sit in my lap. While I was standing up": Marlowe (Humphrey Bogart) and Carmen (Martha Vickers) in **The Big Sleep** (1946).

off each other," she recalled, "particularly the sparring quality. He wanted that to be more evident than it was in the book." Consequently Vivian is once—rather than three times—married, prickly, and playful, rather than pampered and presumptuous, and she seems to turn up everywhere, including places (Joe Brody's apartment, Eddie Mars' hideout) she goes nowhere near in the novel. Furthermore, the absent Regan (with his first name changed from Rusty to Shawn) is no longer her husband; Geiger, though still a blackmailer, is no longer a pornographer nor a homosexual; and Carmen, though still a fruitcake, is no longer a junkie nor a nymphomaniac.

There was one further radical alteration as far as who did what to whom is concerned. Brackett's ending involved a showdown at Geiger's house, with Marlowe inside and Mars, his hoods, and an abundance of weaponry outside. Carmen sneaks in with Marlowe's body in mind. Rejected as she once was by Regan—and this is a girl who finds rejection intolerable—she tries to shoot him with a gun he has had the good sense to unload. As she storms out of the house in disgust, Marlowe turns out the light, and the Mars contingent, seeing only a shadowy figure, guns her down with spectacular conclusiveness. The Production Code officials, who had already frowned at Chandler's original ending, would not tolerate a final scene in which Marlowe is seen to cause Carmen's death. Hawks challenged them to supply a new one and they did, conveniently making Mars the all-round guilty party and paying the price accordingly. "It was a lot more violent," Hawks remarked delightedly. "It was everything I wanted."

He wrote the revised ending with Jules Furthman, Faulkner's collaborator on *To Have and Have Not*, whom he brought in toward the end of the shooting schedule to condense and polish the script. Hawks also changed Faulkner's adaptation of the incident in the novel when Marlowe finds Carmen in his bed, goes into an extended metaphor about chess, sends her packing, and, in an extravagantly melodramatic gesture, tears the bed to pieces. Faulkner's original version of this begins with some light, flirtatious banter that lasts for as long as Marlowe's patience does. When he asks Carmen to leave, she starts biting the white queen from his chess set. In a rage, he slaps her and throws her out. Then he washes his hands, kneels at the fireplace, and hammers the chess piece into a pile of dust. Realizing the potential for comical absurdity that this introduced to an

Marlowe disguised as a bookworm. Agnes (Sonia Darrin) is unimpressed.

otherwise dramatic scene, and wishing in any case to deal briskly with the moment, Hawks rewrote it completely, eliminating the chess element.

He was right, of course. If one is to sidestep Marlowe's obsession with chess, and his concomitant tendency to view the world in terms of its pieces and moves, it is necessary to disregard it entirely. What Faulkner had attempted to find was a cinematic counterpart of the chess analogies that punctuate the novel generally and this chapter in particular: I looked down at the chessboard. The move with the knight was wrong. I put it back where I had moved it from. Knights had no meaning in this game. It wasn't a game for knights." Marlowe has a partiality for knights, and they need not be on a chessboard to

Marlowe is given the once-over by Eddie Mars (John Ridgely, behind) and his stooges.

provide a parallel with his self-image. On the first page of the novel, he is still in the hall of the Sternwood mansion when he notices a stained-glass panel "showing a knight in dark armor rescuing a lady who was tied to a tree and didn't have any clothes on," an apt if hackneyed metaphor for the entire novel.

The final Faulkner-Brackett screenplay was dated October 26, 1944, sixteen days after shooting began. Several weeks later, Faulkner left California. Traveling by train across Arizona and New Mexico on his journey back to Mississippi, he continued work on some sections of the script, which he completed at home. He sent twelve typed pages of rewrites to the studio with a note: "The following rewritten and additional scenes for *The Big Sleep* were done by the author in

Marlowe, Vivian (Lauren Bacall), and Joe Brody (Louis Jean Heydt).

respectful joy and happy admiration after he had gone off salary and while on the way back to Mississippi. With grateful thanks to the studio for the cheerful and crowded day coach, which alone saved him from wasting his time in dull and profitless rest and sleep." One can only speculate on how ironic the tone was intended to be.

Before Faulkner's departure, Chandler was invited over to the Warner lot to meet the principals: Faulkner, Brackett, Hawks, Bogart, and Bacall. "I was just the new kid glad to be working, so he was mostly with the others," Bacall remembered. "He looked like a professor: very quiet, rather shy, quite pleasant. He said nothing memorable, pertinent, or enlightening." Chandler enjoyed the screenplay, particularly Brackett's original ending. He also thought Bogart was

PRIVAT[

636-72

Marlowe,
Canino (Bob
Steele), and
the latter's
silhouette:
"What do
you think it
is, poison?"

the ideal Marlowe. "Bogart can be tough without a gun," he later wrote. "Also, he has a sense of humor that contains that grating undertone of contempt. Alan Ladd is hard, bitter, and occasionally charming, but he is, after all, a small boy's idea of a tough guy. Bogart is the genuine article. Like Edward G. Robinson, all he has to do to dominate a scene is to enter it."

During the filming, Chandler and Hawks remained in occasional contact. The best-known occasion is when Hawks was shooting the scene in which Owen Taylor, the Sternwoods' chauffeur and Carmen's former lover, is pulled out of the ocean after apparently driving the family limousine into it. Hawks, unable to unravel the increasingly sinuous pattern of villainy, sent Chandler a telegram asking who had killed Taylor. Chandler replied that he had no idea. After Jack Warner, who was not interested either way, reproached the waste of money in sending a telegram at all, Hawks never gave him the opportunity to complain about anything else. If Warner or any of his front-office cronies came on the set to check on progress, said Bacall, Hawks simply stopped filming. When they left, he started again. Eventually, the visits stopped.

The plot is certainly confusing, even with the script's modifications. Chandler himself called it "a detective yarn that happens to be more interested in people than plot." Hawks admitted that he could never entirely figure it out.

Behind the credits, a couple stands in silhouette lighting cigarettes, then leave them to burn together in an ashtray. Cigarettes were a particularly significant prop in the films of the Thirties and Forties, their use conveying varying combinations of attraction, camaraderie, obfuscation, nervousness, and procrastination. In *The Big Sleep*, all of these factors are present in Marlowe and Vivian's nicotine-stained romance.

In the opening scene—one of Chandler's finest, intelligently adapted by Faulkner and Brackett—Marlowe visits General Sternwood, a dying old millionaire whose life has come to a standstill and who now spends his waking hours confined to a wheelchair in a greenhouse full of orchids. He has two daughters: Carmen, a thrill-seeking brat in a polka-dot mini-skirt who has already tried to sit on Marlowe's lap ("while I was standing up," the script adds wittily), and Vivian, sardonic, silky, and spoiled. A suspicious book dealer called Geiger is attempting to blackmail Sternwood over "gambling debts" supposedly incurred by Carmen. For his usual twenty-five dollars a day plus expenses, Marlowe agrees to discourage Geiger from applying further pressure. He is also expected to find Shawn Regan, an Irish adventurer who acted as the General's son-substitute and all-purpose companion before disappearing in mysterious circumstances.

When Marlowe meets Vivian, it is an encounter between playful predators. Like him, she is cool, provocative, and smart, providing just the right degree of aphrodisiac competitiveness. Their conversations hum with erogenous promise, a quality to be found in most of Marlowe's collisions with women, however transitory. He dallies behind closed blinds with the bookseller across the road from Geiger's while he waits for him to materialize; he is given a telephone number, with suggestions as to when he should use it, by the female cab driver who, with the immortal words "I'm your girl, bud," helps him to tail a station wagon; he receives appreciative glances from librarians and nightclub hostesses alike. The *Hollywood Reporter* revealed a mixture of awe and envy in its attempt to do justice to his achievements. "It appears," observed an impressed but disgruntled commentator, "that every woman, save one, whom Bogart meets in the course of this drama literally throws herself at him. No man can be that attractive unless the full definition of 'shamus' escapes us."

But it is Vivian alone who ignites his curiosity as much as his libido. One day and two corpses later (Geiger shot while taking candid photographs of Carmen at his house, Taylor drowned behind the wheel of the Sternwood car), she is waiting in his office. "So you do get up," she greets him derisively. "I was beginning to think you worked in bed like Marcel Proust." (Here Chandler supplies the dialogue almost verbatim). "Who's he?" inquires Marlowe, bemused by a literary reference so soon after waking. "You wouldn't know him," she replies with crushing precision. "A French writer." After a prankish interlude of confusing the police-department switchboard together, Marlowe summarizes their respective positions: "You're trying to find out what your father hired me to find out, and I'm trying to find out why you want to find out." "You could go on forever, couldn't you?'" she says, entering into the spirit of the moment. "Anyway, it'll give us something to talk about next time we meet."

In the film version of *The Big Sleep*, it is important that the narrative does not interfere too much in the course of events between Bogart and Bacall. The story may provide the full sentences, but here it is the

Bacall and Bogart: a couple
under siege.

636. 83

punctuation marks which really count. So although it matters to one's comprehension of the plot that in the next scene Marlowe meets Carmen and Eddie Mars at Geiger's house, that Joe Brody is then shot dead by Geiger's boyfriend, Carol Lundgren, and that Marlowe pursues Lundgren and has him arrested, the next *important* scene is the dinner for which Marlowe and Vivian meet after those events are over.

Tellingly, it was added after the film had been cut and scored, and had met with the approval of Warners, which (as a measure of its confidence), decided to delay its release for almost a year so that its appearance could coincide with the Warner "20th Anniversary of Sound on Screen" celebrations. In the interim, Hawks showed the completed film to various groups of American servicemen overseas, whose reactions prompted him to add more episodes of sexily ironic word-play between Bogart and Bacall. When the most notable of them was filmed, Bogart was already in the middle of another picture and Bacall just about to begin one. Written by Jules Furthman, it is an exchange of dialogue that Chandler could easily have written himself, with a chess metaphor, naturally, replacing the equine one:

VIVIAN: What do you usually do when you're not working?
MARLOWE: Play the horses, fool around.
VIVIAN: No women?
MARLOWE: I'm generally working on something most of the time.
VIVIAN: Could that be stretched to include me?
MARLOWE: I like you. I've told you that before.
VIVIAN: I like hearing you say it. You didn't do much about it.
MARLOWE: Well neither did you.
VIVIAN: Well . . . speaking of horses, I like to play them myself. But I like to see them work out a little first, see if they're front runners or come from behind, find out what their whole kind is, what makes them run.
MARLOWE: Find out mine?
VIVIAN: I'd . . .
MARLOWE: Go ahead.
VIVIAN: I'd say you don't like to be rated, you like to get out in front, open up a lead, take a little breather in the back stretch, and then come home free.

MARLOWE: You don't like to be rated yourself.

VIVIAN: I haven't met anyone yet who could do it. Any
      suggestions?

MARLOWE: Well, I can't tell till I've seen you over a
      distance of ground. You've got a touch of class
      but I don't know how far you can go.

VIVIAN: A lot depends on who's in the saddle. Go ahead
      Marlowe, I like the way you move. In case you
      don't know it, you're doing all right.

MARLOWE: There's one thing I can't figure out.

VIVIAN: What makes me run?

MARLOWE: Uh-huh.

VIVIAN: I'll give you a little hint. Sugar won't work. It's
      been tried.

MARLOWE: What did you try it on me for? Who told you
      to sugar me off this case? Was it Eddie Mars?

Pauline Kael once claimed that this dialogue sequence was lifted
from the horse-racing comedy *Straight, Place and Show* (1938), in
which a similar exchange took place between Ethel Merman and
Richard Arlen but, as it lacked the context and the innuendo-laden
delivery of Bogart and Bacall, the resemblance was never mentioned
again. Hawks told Peter Bogdanovich that the scene was prompted
only by the fact that the racing season had begun at Santa Anita and
that, as an enthusiast and the owner of several horses, he considered
it as effective an idea as any of those being proposed.

The consequence of such an enjoyable scene is to make one
anticipate Marlowe and Vivian's next conversation, which follows
soon after at one of Mars's roulette tables and continues during the
car ride home, consistently sabotaged by Marlowe's inconvenient and
ill-timed curiosity. From then on, the film efficiently follows the narrative, with the adjustments already noted and one terrific moment.
Marlowe arranges a meeting with Harry Jones, a small-time hood
played by Elisha Cook Jr., who built a career playing down-at-heel
also-rans. Jones has some information about where Mars's wife is hiding so that everybody will believe she has run off with Regan. The
rendezvous is to occur in an abandoned office building. When
Marlowe walks in, he finds that Canino, one of Mars's henchmen, has
arrived first. As Marlowe watches the silhouetted figures of Canino

and Jones from behind a glass door, a drink in a paper cup is proffered menacingly ("What do you think it is, poison?") before Jones falls to the floor dead.

In the end, Mars, merely a high-class blackmailer in the novel, becomes Regan's killer and an all-round villain. Carmen, once a hopped-up epileptic murderer, is instead just a silly, highly strung victim of circumstance who needs proper care. The siren of an arriving police car provides the musical backdrop for Marlowe and Vivian's concluding clinch.

The Big Sleep is a remarkable film, not least for the evocation of a decaying, wintry Los Angeles it conveys without apparently having left the Warner lot. Paradoxically, while neutralizing the more abrasive elements in Chandler's plot, it compensates for their absence with its own considerable strengths. Chandler should have been pleased, as indeed he was.

Hawks, as always, was giving nothing away. "You're not going to know what to make of this picture," he told a group of critics before the preview. "It holds out its hand for a right-turn signal, then takes a left."

CHAPTER 8

I AM A CAMERA

The Lady in the Lake

At around the time Raymond Chandler began working in Hollywood, Robert Montgomery was dreaming on the high seas. As a U.S. Navy PT boat commander in the South Pacific, he had all the time that was not spent in combat or moving between destroyers to engage in endless purposeful contemplation.

One of his ambitions was to direct. He had made numerous films as an actor since becoming Norma Shearer's urbane flirting partner in the late Twenties, and MGM had been sufficiently eager to complete his transformation into an American Noel Coward to have once given him the Coward role in the screen version of *Private Lives* (1931). Montgomery—though debonair, stylish, and passably counterfeit-English in all the accepted ways—resisted as best he could, concentrating instead on increasing his range as an actor, which he attempted in parts ranging from the killer who carries a head in a hat box in *Night Must Fall* (1937) to the prizefighter who comes down from heaven in *Here Comes Mr. Jordan* (1941).

His aspirations materialized with surprising speed. Returning from the South Seas with a serious case of tropical fever, he recovered sufficiently to co-star with John Wayne in John Ford's naval epic *They*

Were Expendable (1945). When Ford broke his leg, Montgomery took over for the last three weeks of shooting. One could say that it was John Ford's leg that got Robert Montgomery's foot in the door.

Now that he was an accredited if conspicuously inexperienced director, Montgomery made his approach to MGM. His intention, he informed them, was to direct and act in a movie based on John Galsworthy's *Escape* using the subjective camera. The technique was not entirely new. It had been employed before to indicate loss of consciousness on the part of somebody who had fainted, or to suggest a room out of focus for a character who had drunk too much or was experiencing drug withdrawal (one need look no farther than the "spider's web" sequence in *Murder, My Sweet)*. NBC had also used the system for a television adaptation of a radio series, calling the program "First Person Singular," but never before had it been considered as a device for a full-length feature film.

"I wanted to do Galsworthy," said Montgomery, "because the story, people's reactions to an escaped convict, lent itself to the method. I had been contemplating the prospect since before I joined the Navy, but the actual way of doing it, of applying the form as a framework for a whole film, had to be worked out. MGM didn't want to do it, but I persuaded them at least to accept the basic principle. Edward Mannix, the vice-president, eventually gave me the go-ahead to use it in *The Lady in the Lake* when the script was being revised, much to Louis B. Mayer's displeasure—although Mayer was quite happy to accept credit for it after the film had been well-received."

The Lady in the Lake was Chandler's fourth novel and the third to have been adapted from his own short stories—in this case *Bay City Blues, The Lady in the Lake,* and *No Crime in the Mountains.* MGM acquired the film rights to it for $35,000, a sum well over double what he had received for the previous three books put together.

Hired by producer George Haight to write the screenplay, Chandler soon found himself in conflict with the studio over a couch, in circumstances he later described in a letter: "I worked at MGM once in that cold-storage plant they call the Thalberg Building, fourth floor. Had a nice producer, George Haight, a fine fellow. About that time, some potato-brain, probably Mannix, had decided that writers would do more work if they had no couches to lie on. So there was no couch in my office. Never a man to be stopped by trifles, I got a steamer rug out of the car, spread it on the floor, and lay on that. Haight coming in for a courtesy call rushed to the phone and yelled down to the story editor that I was a horizontal writer and for Chrissake send up a couch. However, the cold-storage atmosphere got to me too quick and I said I would work at home. I said a man as big as Mannix should be allowed the privilege of changing his mind. So I worked at home and only went over there three or four times to talk to Haight."

The real problem, however, had nothing to do with the absence of couches or the frostiness of the working climate. It was fostered by the fact that Chandler was so bored with his own material that, instead of doing the orthodox adaptation of the book he had been employed to deliver, he was giving the narrative a complete overhaul. An exasperated Haight, who would have indulged Chandler in any other respect, told him that the studio had bought the property in the first place because they liked it the way it was. He certainly had no wish to debate the issue. Chandler could excuse himself only on the grounds that he had lost interest.

Things rapidly became impossible to resolve. Chandler's contract expired after thirteen weeks, 220 pages (including seventy-five before Marlowe even arrives at the lake), and numerous arguments. The script was revised and completed by Steve Fisher, a studio writer whom Haight assigned to turn Chandler's verbose epic into a 106-page shooting script. "When I had finished it," Fisher remembered, "I took it to Chandler's house for him to see. When he opened the door, I said quite cheerfully, 'Philip Marlowe, I presume.' He didn't like that for some reason and was pretty disagreeable from then on. The fact is that he was incapable of writing a script without a collaborator, although he always complained about having to use one. It was apparent that he didn't like the use of the subjective camera, because he called the studio the next day to tell them that it wouldn't work."

It was the concept itself that he found trite, and this was a contributing factor to his refusal of any credit. "Every young writer or director has wanted to try it," he wrote in 1949. "'Let's make the camera a character'; it's been said at every lunch table in Hollywood one time or another. I knew one fellow who wanted to make the camera the murderer, which wouldn't work without an awful lot of fraud. The camera is too honest."

The idea was that, after an introductory address by Marlowe, everything should be seen through his eyes, the figure behind them only visible when looking in a mirror—as Marlowe sometimes does,

Philip Marlowe (Robert Montgomery) takes a break from the pressure of being a subjective camera. Note the misspelling of "Philip" and "clues": **The Lady in the Lake** (1947).

usually after being beaten up—or at the end, when the lovebirds' crowning clinch is celebrated by a third-person camera. Otherwise, the camera gets to smoke cigarettes, endure police inquiries, fight in hand-to-lens combat, and kiss Audrey Totter, whom Montgomery tested for the female lead after seeing her brief appearance as a perfume salesgirl in a long-forgotten film. She thought she was testing for a version of *Lady* of *the Lake* but got the part anyway because Montgomery assumed that her background in radio would predispose her to play to the microphone. "We had to learn pages of dialogue," she recalled, "because there was no cutting, every scene was complete in itself. I just looked at the camera and pretended it was Marlowe."

Montgomery was well aware of the problems in using the subjective camera: "The main one was to move the camera like the human eye and get the actors to look directly into it, something they were usually trained *not* to do. What we needed was extremely mobile equipment, which MGM didn't have. So we had to move around a lot and use various cameras, under which I'd try to sit as often as possible so that whoever was speaking to the camera would at least have someone to address, even if they did have to look above me."

In addition to making curious changes to the spellings of the characters' names—Marlowe mysteriously acquires an extra "l" in Philip while plain Lieutenant Degarmo becomes a more Gallic-sounding DeGarmot—Fisher made numerous plot modifications. He also decided to set the story at Christmas because, said Montgomery, "it made a nice counterpoint to a murder story."

As carol singing rings out over the credits, a finger moves the greeting cards on which they are printed. Under the final one is a gun. Elegantly groomed, with a crisp white handkerchief in his top pocket, Montgomery delivers his prelude in a style that suggests some head-on collision of Edgar Lustgarten and a passing encyclopaedia salesman, equal parts avuncular crime academic and brilliantined hustler. "My name is Marlowe, Philip [or rather Phillip] Marlowe," he begins. "Occupation: private detective. You know, somebody says, 'Follow that guy.' So I follow him. Somebody says, 'Find that female.' So I find her. And what do I get out of it? Ten bucks a day and expenses . . ."

Understandably, in view of the fact that he has taken a puzzling salary cut of fifteen dollars a day (even in the first novel he never charges less than twenty-five plus expenses), he has started supplementing his negligible income by writing crime stories for pulp magazines. "You'll see it just as I saw it," he promises of the tale he is about to relate. "You'll meet the people; you'll find the clues. And maybe you'll solve it quick and maybe you won't. You think you will, eh? Okay, you're smart."

His story begins three days before Christmas. Laying the foundations for his new career, he had been "pounding out a story (brief pause while he presses two keys on a nearby typewriter) on that" and had sent it to Kingsby Publications, Room 950, Meadsen Building. "Make a note of that," he advises us peremptorily. Somebody called A. Fromsett has written him a letter asking him to visit the company's office, so the whistling subjective camera makes its way along the relevant corridor. In case one has not yet realized that it is three days before Christmas, a passing secretary complains to her companion that "it's three days before Christmas and I haven't done a bit of shopping yet."

In the book, Derace Kingsley runs a cosmetics company. Here he is called Derace Kingsby and, if there were any doubt about what he does, the door to his offices reveals it all: "Lurid Detective Crime Monthly, Monster Stories, Murder Masterpieces, True Horror Tales, Midnight Novelettes." One safely conjectures that he publishes scary trash. Marlowe has arrived to discuss his story "If I Should Die Before I Live," which, unless it happens to be a Murder Masterpiece, would probably be destined for inclusion in the Lurid Detective Crime Monthly. In the event, it is not intended for either. A. Fromsett turns out to be Adrienne Fromsett, played by Audrey Totter, the pop-eyed elasticity of whose performance scans aggressive cordiality, outraged hostility, and simpering helplessness within seconds. Adrienne is giving some poor art editor a hard time when Marlowe enters her office. "No, Dick, it won't do," she admonishes, "not enough gore, not

Marlowe is only seen in a variety of Adrienne Fromsett's (Audrey Totter) mirrors: one in the living room . . .

nearly enough gore." His suggestion that she might be missing some of the intended effect by seeing a monochrome proof is roundly dismissed. "Color or no color, there's not enough blood."

Once Marlowe has settled in front of her desk, we see the first real evidence of what the subjective camera is capable of doing. It sits down, it stands up, it lights a cigarette, it follows a secretary out of the room with a lecherously panoramic gaze. It also speculates correctly—or at least Marlowe behind it does—that Adrienne is not especially interested in his gutter-Dostoyevsky ramblings but rather in employing him as a private detective. She wants him to find Kingsby's wife, Crystal, ostensibly so that the divorce papers can be served. Chandler has Kingsley doing his own hiring, but Fisher's screenplay, building up Totter's part in the style of Bacall's in *The Big Sleep*, gives Adrienne the initiative wherever possible.

. . . and one in the bedroom.

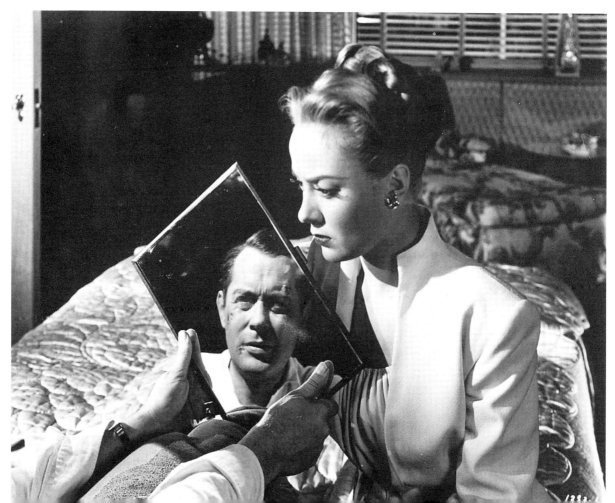

Crystal has apparently absconded with a cartoon of Deep South courtliness called Chris Lavery, whom Marlowe visits at his Bay City house and barely has enough time to marvel at his bogus accent, unremitting smile, and horizontal-striped T-shirt before he finds himself at the business end of a devastating punch. Waking up in jail with a black eye and a spurious drunk-driving charge, Marlowe receives the first of several grillings from the uniformly unpleasant DeGarmot (Lloyd Nolan) and the tough-but-fair Captain Kane (Webber in the novel), played by Tom Tully. Dr. Almore, Lavery's corrupt dope-doctor neighbor who develops into a fundamental part of the novel's mystery, is only a peripheral unseen figure in the movie.

More significant, however, is the omission, except by reference, of the events at Little Fawn Lake where the literary Marlowe visits the Kingsley cabin. He meets the caretaker, Bill Chess, whose wife, Muriel, left him on the same day that Crystal disappeared. In the lake they find Muriel's body—or what is still identifiable of it after thirty days submerged—and Chess is arrested for her murder. Marlowe also discovers that Muriel's real name is Mildred Haviland and that a policeman has recently been in the area looking for her.

All this action, so pivotal to a proper understanding of the narrative, is replaced by two exposition scenes of crucifying dullness, bridged by a brief narration to camera. In one, somebody arrives in Kingsby's office to tell him what has happened, watched by Marlowe. In the other, Marlowe informs Adrienne of what he discovers on his own visit to the lake. All one sees as a substitute for the events themselves is a succession of leaden reaction shots.

After that, Marlowe returns to Lavery's house. There he finds the landlady, Mrs. Fallbrook, with a carnation in her hat and an empty gun she claims to have found on the staircase while dropping in to collect the rent. Lavery, she insists, is nowhere to be found. When she has left, the whistling camera makes its way up to the bedroom. On the dressing table is a handkerchief with Adrienne Fromsett's initials. In the shower is Lavery, slumped in a corner, full of bullet holes.

Marlowe is not welcome when he shows up at Kingsby's office during the company Christmas party. Adrienne is displeased at the notion that she might have killed Lavery. Kingsby is equally displeased at the suggestion that *he* may have killed him. He is also displeased with Adrienne for having hired Marlowe behind his back. Marlowe in turn is displeased with Kingsby for attempting to buy him off.

("Don't think I'm too proud to take it," he snaps, "I'm just too smart to get stuck with it.") Finally, completing the snowballing catalogue of displeasure, Adrienne is displeased with Marlowe for sabotaging her chances with Kingsby. "So you lost me my one million dollars," she whimpers before the carol singing in the background escalates to a degree sufficiently inspirational to restore her self-confidence: "There's more than one Kingsby on the Christmas tree, Mr. Marlowe, and I'll shake one loose yet, don't you worry. And as for you, you're off the case. There isn't any case anymore." But, of course, there is. Unable to tempt Marlowe away from his investigation, Kingsby decides instead to hire him to find Crystal, at the same time taking a rest from the ebullient choristers he employs as his staff.

Marlowe then calls in the Bay City police to examine the Lavery corpse and tells DeGarmot and Kane what he knows. Left alone with DeGarmot, he tells him even more, confronting him with all kinds of pointed speculation about the identity of the policeman who was looking for Mildred Haviland at the lake. They exchange blows, the camera proving dependably resilient. In the novel, Marlowe confines himself to tolerating a provocative slapping; his retaliation here is enough to prompt a visit to police headquarters for interrogation.

It also provides a further opportunity to emphasize how much the Bay City police hate private detectives from Los Angeles. "C'mon, let me work him over," DeGarmot, barely able to contain his eagerness, proposes to Kane before being given the rest of the evening to cool off. Kane himself forsakes whatever minor aspirations toward tough-guy severity he might once have possessed when his attempted questioning of Marlowe is interrupted first by his young daughter then by his wife, both asking when he is planning to return home for Christmas Eve as it is his turn to be Santa. (Fisher, having chosen to give his adaptation a Yuletide setting, was clearly not averse to exploiting the possibilities.)

Christmas Eve, it becomes clear, is a difficult time for everybody. When Adrienne arrives at Marlowe's hotel room to protest her innocence and encourage him to spend the night with her, she receives a very chilly welcome, bordering on no welcome at all. When a preoccupied Marlowe—having discovered that Mildred Haviland once worked for Dr. Allmore when his wife was found dead under mysterious circumstances—visits the late wife's parents, he is shown to the door with a distinct lack of seasonal hospitality. (Chandler's charac-

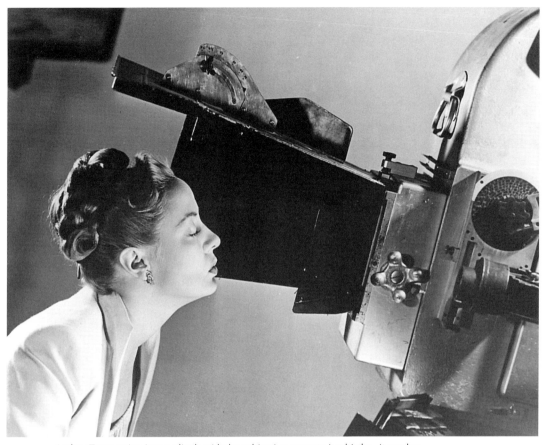

Audrey Totter going into a clinch with the subjective camera: it whistles, it smokes, it fights, it kisses.

ters tell Marlowe everything they know. The parents' attitude in the film has been "borrowed" from an excluded character, Mrs. Tarley, the wife of the investigator they hire to pursue their suspicions.)

When Marlowe leaves their house, the subjective camera finally displays its cinematic virtuosity in a scene of sustained brilliance. Looking in the rear-view mirror of his car as a nightmarish choir invades the soundtrack, he realizes he is being followed. As he accelerates, headlight beams from passing vehicles punctuate the darkness. When his pursuer, by now discernible as DeGarmot, catches up with him and forces him to crash, his car ends up on its side. Hoping for the desired drunk-driving frame-up after the previous frustrated attempt, Dr. DeGarmot pours whisky over Marlowe and goes to call the police. Meanwhile, a reveler on his way home peers into the car. Marlowe knocks him out, leaves his own wallet in the drunk's pocket and, in a tireless display of stumbling and crawling, reaches a phone booth. He tells Adrienne where he is, then collapses, concluding the most effective five minutes in the film.

Marlowe wakes up in Adrienne's apartment. Their association until now has been prickly, to say the least. During his first visit to her love-nest, his attitude is unequivocal: "I have an allergy against getting mixed up with tricky females who want to knock off the boss's wife and marry him for themselves." On the next occasion, he berates her for not being stupid enough: "Why don't you just look beautiful . . . and quit worrying about guns, dead females, and missing ones . . . and that million bucks you want to marry? Start being a woman, quiet down long enough to hear your own heartbeat. You might wake up and find it's a different world."

Marlowe is not welcome at Kingsby's office party. Leon Ames and Audrey Totter are behind the drinks trolley.

This time the love light is on, the joy juices in motion. She is ready to relinquish her predilection for nightclubs, men, and career in favor of being an acquiescent and dutiful companion. Her own leanings subordinated, she encourages Marlowe to abandon detective work and take up writing, in which she promises to coach him. "I want to take care of you," she sighs. "I want to be your girl. That's what I want for Christmas." They kiss. "You close your eyes, too, don't you, darling," she exclaims in wonderment.

The villains: DeGarmot (Lloyd Nolan) and Mildred Haviland (Jayne Meadows).

The next morning, Marlowe is already wearing a dressing gown previously intended for Kingsby; Adrienne continues to refer to him as "darling" with superfluous frequency. As Marlowe's demands for more malted milk begin to give way to the banalities of answering the doorbell, Kingsby arrives to inform him that Crystal has called requesting money. Marlowe agrees to deliver it, taking a handful of Adrienne's rice with which to leave a trail for the police to follow. (Another detail from Fisher's fertile imagination, introduced to compress the novel's rather long-winded ending.)

From then on, the explanations take over. Marlowe confronts "Crystal" with her true identity as Mildred (doubling as Mrs. Fallbrook) and proposes that not only did she kill Crystal but Lavery and Mrs. Allmore as well. (French-speaking spotters of ironic clues might have deduced that Crystal was dead as early as the credits, where the actress playing the role is listed as "Ellay Mort.") "I got into trouble but I'm really a nice girl." Mildred protests feebly as her hysteria swells. "I am nice, aren't I?" "Sure," replies Marlowe stonily, "I'd like to play dolls with you." She is shot by DeGarmot. DeGarmot is shot by the rice-trail police. Marlowe is not shot by anyone.

Instead, he displays suspicious signs of comprehensive infatuation when Adrienne walks into his office with one-way tickets to New York, where he will begin his new career as a pulp writer. "Aren't you scared?" he asks, continuing their by-now standard exchange. "Yes, but it's wonderful," she replies before a triumphant kiss-and-fade. A Christmas card depicting the three wise men announces the end.

Fisher acknowledged that his ending was hackneyed, but Chandler's, he felt, was even worse. He also claims that the film, with a budget of a mere one million dollars, took in four million at the box office in the first month of release.

In some circles, the subjective camera was viewed as the most important development in the cinema since talkies, rather than as the intriguing but stillborn experiment it manifestly is. This is no fault of Montgomery, whose only mistake was to place such disproportionate belief in a technique so ponderous and so loaded with liabilities.

Newsweek certainly fell for it: "After the first few minutes, the illusion is perfect. When Marlowe lights a cigarette, you see his hands extended before the lens that is his face, and the exhaled smoke. When Marlowe is slugged in the jaw by a nervous suspect, it is the camera that is fractured and falls to the floor. But by way of compensation, when Miss Totter kisses Montgomery, it is the lens that takes the rap." The *New Yorker* was less sure: "Substituting for the human eye, the camera constantly fails to realize the limitations of that organ, and it etches into sharp focus all kinds of scenes that the eye could never see clearly." The *New York Times* was less concerned with the camera's failure to duplicate eye movement and more with the fact that Marlowe had too much dialogue for the technique to be properly effective: "To be entirely 'subjective,' the camera character should not talk at all because that destroys the illusion of complete participation by the audience. What is said by this character—this unseen, off-stage voice—may not be at all what people in the audience are thinking or what they would say. As a consequence, the voice takes on a sort of third personality; it comes from another observer who is apparently standing right alongside of you."

The Lady in the Lake was, perhaps significantly, the last film in Montgomery's seventeen-year association with MGM. He moved to Universal, where he directed *Ride the Pink Horse* (1947) and *Once More, My Darling* (1949), neither of them involving the subjective camera, before drifting toward political interests and eventual retirement.

The system he had helped so enthusiastically to pioneer settled into its new status as a useful but limited cinematic device, although, soon after, Delmer Daves employed the subjective camera for the first forty minutes of *Dark Passage* (1947). It was not until the widespread use of hand-held cameras in Hollywood films, and the subsequent invention of the Steadicam, that the technique became fully assimilated, with thrillers and horror movies leading the way.

Films like John Carpenter's *Halloween* (1978) and Sam Raimi's *The Evil Dead* (1982), for example, memorably substitute a roving first-person camera for the murderer one barely sees (unsurprisingly in the latter, as the murderer is a spirit.) In the studio mainstream, many of the movies of Martin Scorsese and Brian De Palma—particularly those made since 1980—have favored a stalking, subjective point of view, which directors such as James Cameron and John McTiernan later assimilated into the visual vocabulary of the action picture.

While its borrowers refined and modified the method, *The Lady in the Lake* now looks exactly what it is: a curio without a cause.

CHAPTER 9

SMALL CHANGE

The Brasher Doubloon
(U.K. title: *The High Window*)

Much in the same manner as RKO had done two years earlier when it disinterred its recently filmed but quickly forgotten literary property *Farewell My Lovely* and made it all over again, in 1946 Fox decided to take the covers off its own Chandler title, *The High Window,* confident that few would remember its previous movie incarnation as *Time to Kill.* Accomplished for less than the cost of a single day's salary for a 1990s star, the film had been tailored to the requirements of the studio's then-popular Michael Shayne series. Philip Marlowe had since proved his appeal as a film character, so his name could now be restored for the remake.

The High Window is not the most engaging of Chandler's novels and Marlowe himself seems depressingly off-form: he even talks to statues. Unlike its predecessors *The Big Sleep* and *Farewell My Lovely*—both of which make extensive use of the short stories that prompted them—it is an "original," Chandler changing his first title *The Brasher Doubloon* to *The High Window* because, he wrote, "it is simple, suggestive, and points to the ultimate essential clue."

Fox's choice of director was John Brahm, formerly Hans Brahm of Hamburg, who had been a theater director and filmmaker in

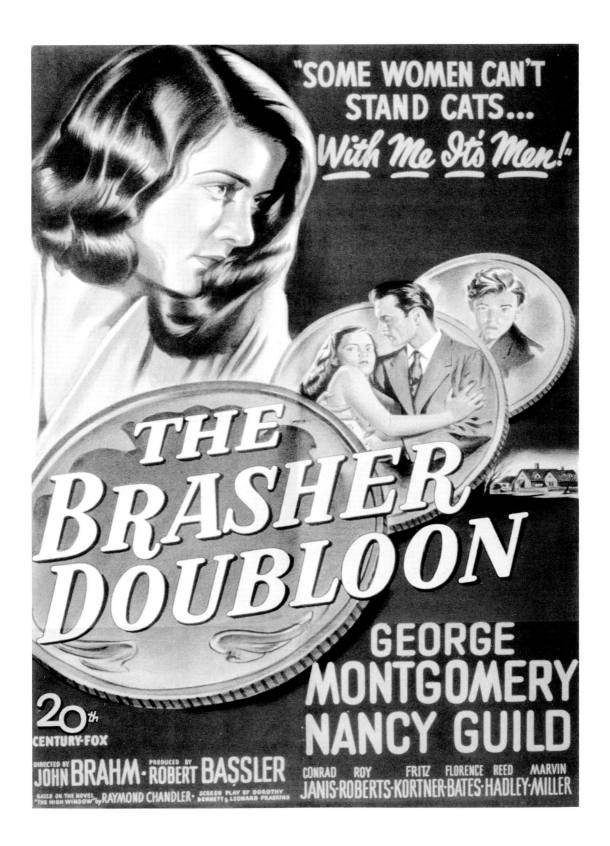

Europe before the time-honored "call from The Coast" brought him to Hollywood. His films *The Lodger* and *Hangover Square* (both 1944—the latter, contrary to suggestion, is not a film about a place where drunks congregate to sleep off their excesses) were successive turn-of-the-century gaslit thrillers that won much acclaim as Fritz Lang-like excursions into Victorian gothic. Both were produced by Robert Bassler, who had already been appointed to do the same on *The Brasher Doubloon*.

Dorothy Hannah, a $1000-a-week contract writer, was given the novel and a salary raise in rapid succession, then told to start work while Bassler and Brahm chose their Marlowe. They decided on George Montgomery. A former stuntman, double for the Lone Ranger, Western hero, and romantic lead in musicals, Montgomery had recently returned from a three-year spell in the Army, and Fox was determined to steer his obvious box-office potential toward more dramatic roles. To this end, he was instructed to sport a moustache, which accounts for the growth resembling a dead caterpillar that is evident on his upper lip throughout the film.

Montgomery—who became a prominent sculptor and furniture maker, talents he developed during his acting years—had a briskly realistic assessment of his own performance: "You have to remember that I came in fresh off the farm in Montana and the next thing I knew I was being touted as the star of the year and the year after. I was going to be a boxer when I came to Hollywood—I had boxed with my brothers, who were both Northwest champions. I had done a number of films by then, but *The Brasher Doubloon* was the first of its kind for me. Mind you, I probably did everything the same— it was a case of being given a part and handed a script. In retrospect, I'd like to have played Marlowe when I was a little older. John Brahm was a marvelous guy but no great shakes as a director. If I'd had Henry Hathaway or Walter Lang or Henry King on it, it might have been different—they would've helped me define the character better. As it stands, it was my own interpretation, and I didn't know a hell of a lot about interpretation. Let's say it wasn't exactly an Academy Award performance." (Dorothy Hannah's evaluation was that "George Montgomery was a soft, sweet man but wrong for Marlowe. He had all the charm but none of the toughness of a private eye.")

The female lead was Nancy Guild, a young actress still in her first year at the University of Arizona when Fox, conducting one of their periodic searches for "the typical American girl," gave her a role in the amnesiac drama *Somewhere in the Night* (1946) and launched her with a publicity campaign built around the phrase "rhymes with wild!" "Before the picture started," wrote Harry Brand, the studio's publicity director, in a protracted puff about *The Brasher Doubloon,* "Nancy broke her engagement to a young director at Warners, realizing she was still too young to be serious about anything other than her career, because she feels she has too much to learn about movies and is not ready for marriage. Nancy dated only once a week while working and no steady romances appeared."

Even younger than Guild and playing Leslie Murdock was Conrad Janis, already a success as a chubby juvenile as well as being, the studio claimed, an art expert with a personal collection of rare paintings independent of his wealthy parents. The Fox front office was concerned about Janis's image. Indeed, they were so apprehensive of eroding his chances as a rakish successor to Tyrone Power— somehow managing to disregard the fact that he looked more like Mickey Rooney—that Linda Conquest, Leslie's estranged wife in Chandler's novel and an integral part of the plot, is, with the uncontested finality of such image-prompted decisions, simply eliminated from the script.

Not content with jettisoning one of the central characters and adjusting the plot to accord with her departure, the liquidation squad moves in on several others. Linda's evocatively named former flatmate, Lois Magic, also disappears, together with any reference to her affair with the blackmailer Vannier or to her marriage to Alex Morny, owner of the swish Idle Valley Club. What can be assumed to be his replacement, Vince Blair, has a small-time crook's Skid Row jazz-joint called the Lucky Club and none of Morny's questionable charm. The policemen (Breeze and Spangler) have their parts reduced to punctuation marks; Hench, Palermo, Teager, and their corresponding subplots do not appear at all. Marlowe's psychiatrist friend, Dr. Moss, played by Reed Hadley and credited on the original cast list (and poster) issued by the studio, has ended up on the cutting-room floor. Even the concluding whodunit has changed, as has much of the motivation leading to it. The cumulative effect is to make one wonder why Fox bothered to remake it. In equating indiscriminate abbreviation with increased comprehensibility, Dorothy Hannah (or Leonard Praskins, who did the adaptation) succeeds

At the Murdock house, Marlowe (George Montgomery, with dead caterpillar on upper lip) meets secretary Merle (Nancy Guild) and son Leslie (Conrad Janis) in **The Brasher Doubloon** (1947).

only in demolishing Chandler's intricate logic, reducing the complex narrative to mere plot mechanics.

The Brasher Doubloon begins promisingly with the familiar narration and the even more familiar big house to which Marlowe has been called. This one is in Pasadena, where a summer wind from the Mojave desert is giving the trees a thorough shaking, as it continues to do throughout the film. Greeted tentatively by the pretty and nervous Merle Davis (Nancy Guild, rhymes with wild), Marlowe is corrected in his assumption that she is the Mrs. Murdock whom he has come to see. As her secretary, Miss Davis hopes he is not disappointed. "I'm disappointed you're not my client," he quips inanely, "but the Miss makes up for it."

Like previous movie Marlowes, this incarnation also considers it mandatory to make romantic overtures to any female character within a ten-year age gap. Despite the ornamental larva on his upper lip, Montgomery's Marlowe is not shy about making passes, or slow in getting around to it, but he belabors his attempts at seduction, and his occasional wit has a starchily rehearsed quality. He is handsome, vapid, colorlessly aggressive: one can tell he is going to be no fun.

Merle advises him that Mrs. Murdock is "a little difficult and rather eccentric" but otherwise harmless. First, however, he meets her son Leslie (Conrad Janis, doesn't rhyme with Power) in a neatly scripted scene added by Hannah. Leslie has just finished telling Marlowe that his mother does not require his services when the summons comes through from the lioness's den. "You must've forgotten to tell your mother she didn't want to see me," says Marlowe impassively—one of the few new lines in the film that is worthy of Chandler.

The parlor in which Mrs. Murdock receives him is like an equatorial rain forest with furniture. It contains almost as many plants as General Sternwood's hot house in *The Big Sleep*. Unlike Sternwood, the bossy, cantankerous old gargoyle does not permit Marlowe to smoke, on account of a respiratory condition, but hires him, at his customary rate of twenty-five dollars a day plus expenses, to recover a rare doubloon missing from her safe. Given the studio's reluctance to allow Leslie a wife, there is no disaffected daughter-in-law for her to blame, so her suspicions are confined to Leslie and Merle, the only people other than herself who know the combination number.

Marlowe is visited by Eddie Prue (Alfred Linder), a stooge in a straw hat.

Mrs. Murdock's manner is not only tetchy but cagey. This eventually exasperates Marlowe, who—consonant with the screenplay's overall tendency to subordinate narrative thrust to opportunities for "love interest"—refuses to take the case, only recovering his curiosity after Merle reveals her own problem: she hates to be touched by men. "It's a phobia I get," she explains, adding promisingly: "That doesn't mean I wouldn't like to get over it." His professional inquisitiveness increased further by the presence of a gun in her desk drawer, he accepts both assignments.

Marlowe returns to his office and tosses his hat with practiced expertise straight onto a peg on the coat stand. He is visited by a stooge in a straw hat called Eddie Prue, representing the sinister club owner Vince Blair, who, in the usual manner, attempts to discourage Marlowe from pursuing his investigation. (People attempting to discourage him from pursuing an investigation are as fundamental to Marlowe's routine as big houses in Pasadena and beautiful, devious women.) Eddie Prue is unsuccessful in his mission, the lapels of his jacket curling up in defeat.

Next, Marlowe goes to see Elisha Morningstar, an old coin dealer who, by calling Mrs. Murdock about the doubloon, has first attracted

Merle requests treatment for her man phobia.

her concern about its possible loss. He is chronically unhelpful. Making leaving noises (receding footsteps, closing of door), Marlowe overhears him calling a private detective, George Anson (George Anson Phillips in the novel), whose apartment he decides to visit. "The Florence Apartments," says Montgomery's voice-over (evocatively paraphrasing Chandler), "was a rooming house on Bunker Hill, which was the choice place to live in Los Angeles. Nowadays, people live there because they haven't any choice." Marlowe finds him dead, which he reports to the police. He also finds a baggage-claim ticket, which he does *not* report to the police but instead exchanges for a package containing the doubloon.

Returning to Morningstar's, Marlowe finds that he, too, has joined the traditional trail of corpses with—as an auxiliary red herring—the gun from Merle's desk drawer lying beside him. Anxious to verify its authenticity, Marlowe breaks into the Murdock house and, in a succession of scenes so leaden that they would require the voltage of an entire power station to bring them to life, meets first Merle, who informs him that the doubloon has been found and his assignment concluded; then Leslie, who claims he stole it to pay a gambling debt but returned it when the threat of disinheritance proved too upsetting; and finally, the old dragon herself ("Merle, do I hear that man Marlowe in there? Well send him in *here*!"). As the shadows of wind-blown trees flicker behind him—for all its liabilities, the film always looks as good as Brahm movies invariably do—Marlowe is told of the apparent link between Merle's instability and the fact that Mrs. Murdock's husband fell to his death from an office window (her only deceased husband in the film but the first of two in the novel). When Marlowe shows them the doubloon they are all claiming has been returned, there is collective apoplexy.

Next to join the jigsaw is Vannier, a twitchy little weasel who, after being subjected to Marlowe's hat-and-stand trick, makes it apparent how much he wants the doubloon by pointing a gun at Marlowe. Marlowe is unimpressed and has little problem in disarming him, punctuating his speech with uncharacterisitic exclamations like "For the love of Mike!" and—when he notices an increase in Vannier's excitability as he tosses the coin—"This thing really sends you, doesn't it!" Discovering that Vannier is a news cameraman, Marlowe decides that he is blackmailing someone with film he has shot.

It does not take him long to find out who it is. Merle is waiting at his apartment. Like everybody else in the picture, she wants the doubloon, but she is also anxious to overcome her physical problem with men. "What about this phobia of yours?" asks Marlowe, unable to conceal his delight at her willingness. "It's responding to treatment already," she purrs, eyes closed, lips puckered. Coming up for air, she explains the situation. She was secretary to Mrs. Murdock's ruttish husband, who used to harass her; while they were watching the Tournament of Roses parade five years earlier (eight in the book), he miscued a grope and fell out of the office window; since then, she has sacrificed herself to guilt and Mrs. Murdock has been paying Vannier substantial hush money to suppress the piece of film that records the event. (It is typical of the film's generally contrived nature that a photograph in the novel should arbitrarily be changed to newsreel footage.) Like the other doubloon seekers, Merle pulls out a gun, but Marlowe dupes her into handing it over, and she is back in his arms in a matter of moments. A nicely played scene, this—nothing to do with Chandler, but nor has much else in the film.

On his way out to sleep at the office—the introductory lessons in sexual response have gone far enough for one evening—Marlowe is bundled into a car and taken to the Lucky Club, the same tavern set on the Fox lot where (before the substitution of wooden benches, tankards, and cleavage by leather chairs, cocktail glasses, and lounge lizards) Cornel Wilde had met Linda Darnell in the period drama *Forever Amber* only a few months before.

There, Blair and his cronies, including Leslie, are ready to ask a few questions. Everybody, it seems, is after the doubloon. When Marlowe proves uncooperative, he is beaten up, his vulnerability emphasized by the routine but always effective low-angle shot of his aggressors. Inexplicably, having conferred several disagreeable bonus blows when they realize he is listening in on their bickering, the assailants apply soothing cold compresses a moment later. Capitalizing on their internal squabble, Marlowe engineers a fight among them and dives through a window, his escape assisted unwittingly by a cluster of Skid Row drunks to whom he announces the proximity of an open wine barrel. In their rush to find it, they prevent Marlowe's pursuers—who are fewer in number and not nearly so desperate—from making much progress.

Back at his office the following morning, Marlowe receives a call from Merle. She is at Vannier's home, she explains; he is dead and

The final confrontation: Mrs. Murdock (Florence Bates), Marlowe, and Merle.

she is worried. At the house, with Merle pleading innocent and the wind blowing even more ferociously than usual, Marlowe finds the film that Vannier has been employing as his long-term meal-ticket. Assuming it will incriminate her, Merle tries to burn it. It is rescued by Leslie, newly arrived with gun in hand. When it is safely in Marlowe's, the police are called.

The interested parties congregate at Marlowe's office for an explanation of who did what to whom. Leslie has confessed to bumping off Anson and Morningstar, despite the fact that Chandler made Vannier responsible for both murders in the novel. Mrs. Murdock is still trying to blame Merle for everything, for reasons that become apparent when Marlowe projects Vannier's film. An enlarged frame clearly shows Mrs. Murdock pushing her soon-to-be-late husband out of his office window—or as Marlowe himself so poetically describes it, "Here we have Mrs. Murdock in the act of giving her husband the old heave-ho." Mrs. Murdock is also revealed to have killed Vannier,

"Here we have Mrs. Murdock in the act of giving her husband the old heave-ho."

which Leslie does in the novel. Marlowe and Merle are left to continue the desensitization treatment, the prospects improved immeasurably by the knowledge that Merle's problem had its origins in something she never did. "I've got a feeling you're going to graduate with honors," coos Marlowe before treating her to a potentially traumatizing tongue sandwich.

If studio mythology is to be believed, this was George Montgomery's 1037th line in the film and the conclusion of his 464th separate speech, second only in Fox's history at the time to Alexander Knox's 1127 lines in *Wilson* (1944). The *New York Times* thought George Montgomery's problem was the same as Robert Montgomery's: he was excessively clean-cut and insufficiently rugged. The *Hollywood Reporter* was dutifully approving, referring to Montgomery's performance as "forthright," but generally it was acknowledged that he was a little too smooth and petulant to carry it off with any real conviction. Alton Cook, for example, thought that "Philip Marlowe has been slipping out of his mood of witty cynicism into a mere bad-tempered insolence. At the hands of George Montgomery, he gets the loudest and surliest treatment of all."

Several assessments, incomprehensibly, bordered on the eulogistic. "A mighty faithful translation, catching the spirit and blood and thunder of the original," wrote one deranged periodical. Having little to do with Chandler other than in the rudiments of its plot outline, supplemented by a vague nod toward his style, *The Brasher Doubloon* is not "a mighty faithful translation" or anything approaching it. And when *Films in Review* later deemed it to be "the least violent, moodiest, and perhaps finest U.S. private eye feature," one can only conclude that the magazine's wish to be complimentary in its retrospective look at John Brahm's career as an *auteur* blinded it to the film's massive shortcomings.

Time was discreetly favorable: "These whodunit movies are fast running to formula, but the chances are that in at least two respects they will continue to be better than most movies: 1) in their portrayal of the shabby, menacing beauty of U.S. cities [there is a breathtaking street view of a Los Angeles rooming house in *Doubloon*] and 2) in the minor players who, with only a minute or so to make their points, impersonate, with passionate proficiency, the deep-sea fish of the underworld."

The public, as ever, voted with their money. *The Brasher Doubloon* opened at the Roxy in New York in the same program as Jack Benny's vaudeville show. The record takings that followed were plainly not prompted by the presence of the feature film. A headline in *Variety* said it all: DOUBLOON SMALL CHANGE COMPARED TO COMIC'S DRAW.

CHAPTER 10

THE END OF THE AFFAIR

Strangers on a Train

La Jolla was, and from all accounts still is, a prosperous, pleasant, clean, quiet suburb of San Diego. In 1946, Chandler and his wife, Cissy, moved into 6005 Camino de la Costa. He was fifty-eight and exhausted; she was seventy-five and constantly ill.

They enjoyed a discreet, secluded, ritualistic life, lunching together and taking tea in the afternoon with the curtains drawn to soften the glare of the sun descending over the Pacific. She went to bed early while he read and wrote the letters that had become his communication cord to the outside world. Their social life was uneventful. Occasionally they entertained a few friends, or Chandler received a brief visit from business colleagues who had traveled down from Los Angeles. Otherwise, they may as well have been living in Tierra del Fuego.

Chandler's hatred for Hollywood was as unswerving as ever. Writing to Alfred Knopf at the beginning of the year, he described it as "a degraded community whose idealism even is largely fake. The pretentiousness, the bogus enthusiasm, the constant drinking and drabbing, the incessant squabbling over money, the all-pervasive agent, the strutting of the big shots (and their usually utter incompe-

YOU'LL BE IN THE GRIP OF LOVE'S STRANGEST TRIP!

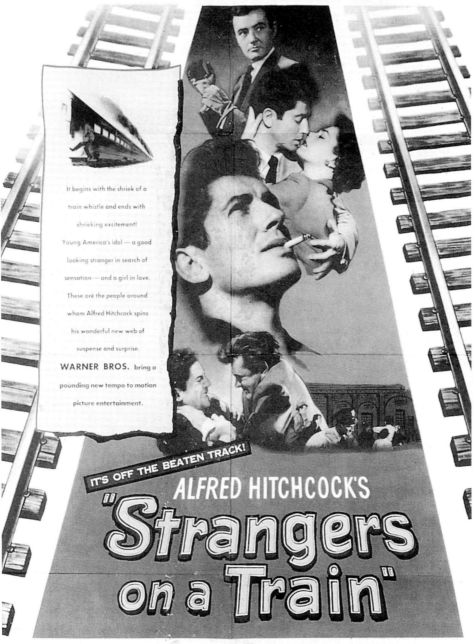

It begins with the shriek of a train whistle and ends with shrieking excitement! Young America's idol — a good looking stranger in search of sensation — and a girl in love. These are the people around whom Alfred Hitchcock spins his wonderful new web of suspense and surprise. **WARNER BROS.** bring a pounding new tempo to motion picture entertainment.

IT'S OFF THE BEATEN TRACK!

ALFRED HITCHCOCK'S
"Strangers on a Train"

STARRING **FARLEY GRANGER** **RUTH ROMAN** **ROBERT WALKER**

with LEO G. CARROLL · Screen Play by RAYMOND CHANDLER and CZENZI ORMONDE · A Warner Bros. Pictures tence to achieve anything they start out to do), the constant fear of losing all this fairy gold and being the nothing they have never really ceased to be, the snide tricks, the whole damn mess is out of this world . . . it is like one of those South American palace revolutions conducted by officers in comic-opera uniforms—only when the thing is over, the ragged dead men lie in rows against the wall, and you suddenly know that this is not funny, this is the Roman circus, and damned near the end of civilization."

A return visit to see his new West Coast agent, Ray Stark, served merely to reinforce this impression: "These Hollywood people are fantastic when you have been away for a while. In their presence, any calm, sensible remark sounds faked. Their conversation is a mess of shopworn superlatives interrupted by four telephone calls to the sentence."

By 1947, his increasingly weary hero, Philip Marlowe, had become a radio sleuth, first on NBC with Van Heflin as the audio gumshoe, then a year later in a long-running CBS series featuring Gerald Mohr. Chandler was unhappy about the prospect of his creation being employed as a vehicle for half-hour serial-style broadcasts. But he needed the money and, after initially insisting on script approval, conceded even on that score. He may have comforted himself with the knowledge that the format had already worked for Dashiell Hammett's Sam Spade and Erle Stanley Gardner's Perry Mason, but one doubts it. Television also semaphored its interest, but Chandler's demands, prompted and compounded by his dislike of the new medium, were to delay any further developments until his final years.

Also in 1947, he signed a contract with Universal in what he described as "one of the most unusual deals ever made in Hollywood, or so I am told. They pay me a large sum of money and a percentage of the picture to write them a screenplay, and they only get the picture rights. The unusual feature is that they do not employ me, but merely agree to buy the motion picture rights to something I write in my own way and without any supervision."

The screenplay was *Playback*, the rudiments of which would later be recycled into his last and least distinguished novel. The large sum of money was $4000 a week. William Dozier and Joseph Sistrom, two of the few Paramount executives for whom Chandler had retained any regard, were now at Universal, and their presence there was a contributing factor to his acceptance of the offer. He had already begun work on a new Philip Marlowe book, his first for several years, to be called *The Little Sister*. This would clearly have to be delayed.

Working at home as he now demanded, Chandler found scriptwriting on his own as enervating as he had with *The Blue Dahlia*. "I finished the first draft of my screenplay," he wrote to Hamish Hamilton, "and the way I went on, anyone would think I was building a pyramid . . . Now I have to polish it, as they say. Which means leave out half and make what is left hammier. This is a very delicate art, and about as fascinating as scraping teeth."

After completing his 224-page script, Chandler was jaded and grouchy. He complained assiduously: about his house, which was too expensive; about the domestic staff, who were either unreliable or unavailable; and about Cissy's debilitated condition, which was an invariable source of worry. Everything seemed to be wrong, as it so often was for him. Eventually, financial difficulties at Universal, exacerbated by the mounting costs of the required location shooting in Vancouver, pressured the studio to cut its potential losses and abandon the project. Chandler returned to *The Little Sister*.

In July 1950, he was approached by Warner Bros. to write a screenplay, at a salary of $2500 a week for five weeks' work, from Patricia Highsmith's newly published novel *Strangers on a Train*, to be directed by Alfred Hitchcock.

"Together with Barbara Keon, the associate producer, I flew from Los Angeles to San Diego, took a limousine to La Jolla, and spent the afternoon in discussion with him." Hitchcock, with his customary regard for detail, was describing the beginning of his brief and blemished association with Chandler. The problem became apparent from the start: Chandler insisted on working without interruption or interference while Hitchcock wanted to make a contribution to the writing of the script he would eventually be directing. He was even prepared to travel to Chandler's house to do so.

On August 17, Chandler wrote a letter to Ray Stark: "Hitchcock seems to be a very considerate and polite man, but he is full of little suggestions and ideas, which have a cramping effect on a writer's initiative. You are in a position of a fighter who can't get set because he is continuously being kept off balance by short jabs. I don't complain about this at all. Hitchcock is a rather special kind of director. He is always ready to sacrifice dramatic logic (insofar as it exists) for the sake of a camera effect or a mood effect. He is aware of this and accepts the handicap. He knows that in almost all his pictures there is some point where the story ceases to make any sense whatsoever and becomes a chase, but he doesn't mind. This is very hard on a writer, especially on a writer who has any ideas of his own, because the writer not only has to make sense out of the foolish plot, if he can, but he has to do that and at the same time do it in such a way that any kind of camera shot or background shot that comes into Hitchcock's mind can be incorporated into it."

On September 4, it was Hamish Hamilton's turn to receive a progress report: "It's a silly story and quite a chore. Why am I doing it? Partly because I thought I might like Hitch, which I do, and partly because one gets tired of saying no, and someday I might want to say yes and not get asked. . . . The thing that amuses me

The strangers in question: Guy (Farley Granger) and Bruno (Robert Walker) in **Strangers on a Train** (1951).

about Hitchcock is the way he directs a film in his head before he knows what the story is . . . His idea of characters is rather primitive: Nice Young Man, Society Girl, Frightened Woman, Sneaky Old Beldame, Spy, Comic Relief, and so on. But he is as nice as can be to argue with."

Patricia Highsmith's novel provided an intriguing if unlikely premise. Guy Haines, an enterprising young architect whose unfaithful wife has become pregnant by another man, is engaged in conversation aboard a train by an Oedipal screwball called Charles Bruno who suggests that, as he hates his father and learns that Guy is unhappy with his wife, they should swap murders since neither would be suspected of the other's crime. "A pure murder," Bruno later ruminates ecstatically in an El Paso hotel room, "without personal motives!" Despite Guy's lack of interest in the scheme, Bruno fulfills his part by killing Guy's wife, and he expects the gesture to be reciprocated.

Much of the remaining narrative was compressed significantly by Whitfield Cook, who did the initial film adaptation before Chandler and Hitchcock began work on the screenplay. The locations—which in Highsmith cover Texas, Mexico, Florida, and all around New York—are confined to Metcalf (Guy's home town, which here is somewhere between Washington and New York rather than in Texas), Washington itself, and Forest Hills, where Guy plays tennis during the climactic half-hour of the film. The fact that Guy has been transformed into a well-known tennis player makes it simpler and more plausible for Bruno (now called Bruno Anthony) to know about aspects of Guy's life without needing to pry. In the film, it is a cigarette lighter (of which Hitchcock will make an effective dramatic prop) that Guy leaves in Bruno's compartment rather than a book by Plato, while his girlfriend's father becomes a senator in consonance with the Washington setting. More significantly, Guy does not kill Bruno's father, as he does in the novel, after some agonizing. Much of the overall elementary psychology has also evaporated—understandably, considering film's general resistance to it as a medium—together with the more obvious thrill-of-the-kill parallels with Richard Fleischer's *Compulsion* (1957) and Hitchcock's own *Rope* (1948).

Chandler had particular difficulty working out a scene in which Guy appears to be keeping his (unwilling) part of the bargain by murdering Bruno's father, and voiced it in the form of notes:

(1) A perfectly decent young man agrees to murder a man he doesn't know, has never seen, in order to keep a maniac from giving himself away and from tormenting the nice young man.

(2) From a character point of view, the audience will not believe the nice young man is going to kill anybody, or has any idea of killing anybody.

(3) Nevertheless, the nice young man has to convince Bruno and a reasonable percentage of the audience that what he is about to do is logical and inevitable. This conviction may not outlast the scene, but it has to be there, or else what the hell are the boys talking about?

(4) While convincing Bruno of all this, he has yet to convince him utterly so that some suspicion remains in Bruno's mind that Guy intends some kind of trick, rather than to go through with it in a literal sense.

(5) All through this scene (supposing it can be written this way), we are flirting with the ludicrous. If it is not written and played exactly right, it will be absurd. The reason for this is that the situation actually is ludicrous in its essence, and this can only be overcome by developing a sort of superficial menace, which really has nothing to do with the business at hand.

(6) Or am I still crazy?

Chandler and Hitchcock continued their uneasy collaboration. "Eventually it became clear to me that it wasn't going to work," Hitchcock recalled. "I would suggest a way of doing something and he would reply 'Well, if you can figure it out, what do you need me for?'"

Time passed. On September 27, Chandler wrote another note to Ray Stark: "I haven't even spoken on the telephone to Hitchcock since the 21st August, when I began to write the screenplay, which was written in one day over five weeks. Not bad for a rather plodding sort of worker like myself. I don't know whether he likes it, or whether he thinks it stinks. The only method I have of deducing an answer to this question is that I was allowed to finish it."

Chandler, it appears, was unable to make up his mind about what degree of involvement was permissible from a collaborator. Hitchcock's had clearly crossed the border that divided excessive interest (at the beginning) and apparent indifference (at the end). Having received no appreciation or acknowledgement, Chandler's disapproval was as inevitable as the aggrieved tone with which he expressed it. When he discovered that Warner had put him on suspension the day before he finished the screenplay, his disgust was complete. His association with Hollywood was to finish as acrimoniously as it had begun.

Meanwhile, Hitchcock was wasting no time. He had already decided that Farley Granger should play Guy. Impressed by his performance as one of the two homicidal young homosexuals in *Rope* under his direction three years earlier, Hitchcock saw him as the perfect unwilling participant in Bruno's aberrant scheme and "borrowed" him from Samuel Goldwyn, to whom Granger was under contract as a romantic lead. Robert Walker, also on loan (from MGM) was cast as Bruno, the dramatic catalyst, the all-*too*-willing participant. (Walker, among the outstanding film actors of his generation, died at the age of thirty-seven, a few months after the completion of *Strangers on a Train*.)

As Granger's affluent, sympathetic girlfriend Anne Morton, Hitchcock chose Ruth Roman, who had once unsuccessfully applied for the part Ingrid Bergman eventually played in *Spellbound* (1945). "The role of the aristocrat," gushed the studio press release, "is to Miss Roman's liking, permitting her to wear a smart, new, short hairdo and some style-setting clothes designed by Leah Rhodes, studio fashion creator." Others in the cast would include Hitchcock's 22-year-old, RADA-trained daughter Patricia as Roman's suspicious and significantly bespectacled younger sister, and Leo G. Carroll as their father.

Next, Hitchcock called in Czenzi Ormonde, a script of whose he had read and liked. He informed her that he was about to make *Strangers on a Train* and that he wanted her to write the screenplay. "When he told me Raymond Chandler had worked on it," she remembered, "I wondered what I was doing there, being a great fan of Mr. Chandler's." Hitchcock explained that his involvement with Chandler was over. Assuming that all that might be required were a few revisions, Ormonde asked to see what he had submitted. Hitchcock picked up Chandler's manuscript, held it between thumb and forefinger over the wastepaper basket, and let it drop. "Now," he said emphatically, savoring the resultant pause, "we start with page one."

"Mr. Hitchcock had an urgent time schedule imposed on him by the front office," said Ormonde, "one of his abominations along with policemen and confrontations. Almost two weeks after I began the script, he left for the East to shoot exteriors with several of the stars. He liked what was happening with the story and felt confident he would approve of what was written while he was gone. He did. He particularly enjoyed the build-up I'd given to Bruno's mother and sent to London for Marion Lorne to play the part."

In singular Hitchcock style, *Strangers on a Train* begins with a collision of feet by two men about to board a train. One is wearing tweed trousers and sensible shoes; the other, striped slacks and the footwear of an untrustworthy character. We have not yet seen their faces, but already we know a little about them. The first is tennis

"I like them to look just right": Mother (Marion Lorne) does Bruno's (Robert Walker) nails.

151.

player Guy Haines (Granger), who is personable, sober, ambitious. The second is Bruno Anthony (Walker), who is garrulous, parasitic, strange. Well, more than strange—a complete psychopath, as it turns out. Within minutes they are talking over lunch. For all of Bruno's numerous problems, shyness with strangers is not among them. He hates his father, to the extent of frequently wanting to kill him. He enjoys danger. ("Have you ever driven a car blindfolded at 150 miles an hour?" he asks, adding unnecessarily, "I have." He has also, he reveals without prompting, traveled in a jet plane and plans to make a reservation on the first rocket to the moon. So far, so harmless.)

It is when he begins to lean forward in a confidential, conspiratorial fashion and display an excessive familiarity with Guy's personal life—his wish to divorce estranged wife Miriam and marry senator's daughter Anne—that Bruno's craziness takes a sinister turn. He wants them to exchange murders. "What is a life or two, Guy?" he asks. "Some people are better off dead. Like your wife and my father, for instance."

Conspicuously relieved by the train's arrival at his station, Guy climbs off as Hitchcock—making his by-now statutory appearance and continuing the sequence of carrying a violin (*Spellbound*) and cello (*The Paradine Case*)—boards the train holding a double bass approximately the same size and shape as himself. Guy's visit to conclude divorce arrangements with Miriam is not a success, as everyone in the music store where she works is compelled to notice. "I'd like to break her foul, useless little neck," he tells Anne on the telephone, a line so idiosyncratically bad tempered that one assumes it was rescued from Chandler's screenplay in Hitchcock's litter bin.

Bruno, meanwhile, is having a marvellous time lying around in his dressing gown getting his nails manicured by his mother (Marion Lorne). "I like them to look just right," he informs her as she concludes her pampering. Mother obviously thinks Bruno is looking a little peaky. "You're so pale, dear. Are you out of vitamins?" He reassures her. "Well, I do hope you've forgotten about that silly little plan of yours," she continues.

"Which one?" he asks, bespeaking the extravagant schemes he hatches every day. She can barely bring herself to reply: "About . . . um . . . blowing up the White House." Clearly a little dotty herself, mother treats Bruno like the mischievous little brat she thinks he is. He laughs uproariously at a painting she is completing that looks like some grisly death's head; he considers it a prodigious representation of his father. "Is it?" she inquires hesitantly, wondering whether she should be offended. "I was trying to paint St. Francis."

When Bruno steps off the train in Metcalf, one suspects that earlier his mind was not entirely on his manicure. Robert Walker's urbanely menacing presence leaves us in no doubt. As he stalks Miriam and her companions around a fairground, his intentions are unmistakable; her interest in him merely facilitates access. Much as he does in all of his films where set pieces are concerned, Hitchcock now turns up the volume of his virtuosity. In the tunnel of love, Miriam screams as Bruno's shadow, following in the boat behind, appears to overtake hers. As he strangles her on the island, the murder is reflected in her glasses, which have fallen on the grass. Before the killing,

The murder reflected in the victim's glasses.

Bruno bursts a child's balloon with his cigarette; after it, he helps a blind man cross the road.

From then on, Hitchcock is wearing his suit of lights, punctuating the film with such a dazzling abundance of visual flourishes that plausibility becomes a peripheral consideration—never dismissed, but always eclipsed. When Guy returns home, Bruno calls him from across the street; under the street lights, he triumphantly shows him the crushed remains of Miriam's spectacles as evidence of his success. Bruno begins to shadow Guy to encourage him—quite reasonably, he feels—to fulfill his part of the putative bargain. One day, Guy sees him standing darkly on the steps of Washington's Jefferson Memorial, his saturnine smallness thrown into relief by the pearly enormity of the building. On another occasion, Guy is sitting by a tennis court watching a practice match when he observes all the heads in the crowd swivelling to follow the ball, except for Bruno's, which is staring straight at him. (During all this time, it should be added, the police are suspicious of Guy, who—inevitably, given the amount of rail travel in the film—was on a train at the time Bruno was murdering his wife. Unlike Walter Neff in *Double Indemnity*, whose fellow passenger in the observation car inconveniently remembers him, Guy's companion, a boozed-up professor from Delaware Tech, inconveniently forgets him. "When an alibi is full of bourbon, it can't stand up," observes Guy in what one speculates to be another Chandler line rescued from the trashcan.)

Among the remaining carnival of effects (cross-cutting between Guy playing a tennis match under police observation at Forest Hills and Bruno attempting to retrieve from a drain the cigarette lighter he intends to plant at the scene of the crime; the finale on an out-of-control merry-go-round), there is one consummate scene whose effectiveness does not rely on the Hitchcock box of tricks. Bruno has ingratiated himself into Senator Morton's party and strides up to the fastidious but imperturbable host to introduce himself. "I'd like to talk to you some time about my idea for harnessing the life force," he begins. "It'll make atomic power look like the horse and buggy. I'm already developing my faculty for seeing millions of miles. And senator, can you imagine being able to smell a flower on the planet Mars?" He takes his leave. "Unusual personality," remarks the senator, whose power of understatement is matched by his ability to detect a fruitcake. Bruno, however, has not quite finished. He persuades a charm-

Bruno passes out at Senator Morton's (Leo G. Carroll) party.

ing old lady (Norma Varden) to offer her neck for what she assumes to be a harmless demonstration of basic strangling techniques. Seeing Anne's sister, whose glasses remind him of Miriam, he presses too hard before unceremoniously passing out.

When filming had finished, the only other matter to be resolved was that of the screenplay credit. Czenzi Ormonde recalled Hitchcock returning from a long meeting with Warner Bros.: "It is the first time I ever saw Mr. Hitchcock perturbed or heard a tremor in his voice. He was furious, he told me. He had argued with the front office because he wanted me to have sole credit on the picture and they insisted, for whatever reasons of their own, that Raymond Chandler have his name on the picture and that it should come first. I was not

Drinks all round as Guy explains his position: (l to r) Leo G. Carroll, Ruth Roman, Farley Granger, Patricia Hitchcock.

about to make a big to-do over whose name came first or gather what energy I had not spent on writing the film to fight for any self-aggrandizement. I let the credit stand the way they wanted it.'

Chandler's attitude was revealed in two letters written on the same day. In the first, he outlined his dilemma: "I ought to refuse credit in connection with such a poor job, but for professional reasons and for the record, and because I haven't had a screen credit for several years, I may have to take whatever credit I'm entitled to. A very sickening situation." In the second, he simply rationalized his position: "The fallacy of this operation was my being involved in it at all, because it is obvious to me now, and must have been obvious to many people long since, that a Hitchcock picture must be all Hitchcock. A script that shows any signs of a positive style must be obliterated or changed until it is quite innocuous, even if that means making it quite silly . . . Stark seemed to enjoy suggesting that my script was bad. But it wasn't bad. It was far better than what they finished with. It just had too much Chandler and not enough Hitchcock."

He settled for a shared credit. He didn't like the film.

The finale on an out-of-control merry-go-round.

CHAPTER 11

SLEUTH WITH A SUNTAN

Marlowe

Eighteen years passed before Chandler's name reappeared in the cinema, and by then he had been dead for ten of them. With television, he was to have a single—largely unconsummated—twilight-years flirtation. Toward the end of 1958, he was approached by two NBC producers, Mark Goodson and Bill Todman, requesting his permission to use the character Philip Marlowe in a TV series of that name, and to adapt and paraphrase Chandler material to the requirements of the individual programs. Uncharacteristically, he agreed.

Chandler's attitude toward television was comparable to his regard for Hollywood: he detested it with the kind of distinctive relish W.C. Fields had once reserved for children and water. As early in its development as 1950, he had declared his view: "To me, television is just one more facet of the considerable segment of our civilization that never had any standard but the soft buck."

What he seemed to abhor in particular was the effortlessness involved in watching it: "You turn a few knobs, a few of those mechanical adjustments at which the higher apes are so proficient, and lean back and drain your mind of all thought. And there you are, watching the bubbles in the primeval ooze. You don't have to concentrate. You don't have to react. You don't have to remember. You don't miss your brain because you don't need it. Your heart and liver and lungs continue to function normally. Apart from that, all is peace and quiet. You are in the poor man's nirvana. And if some nasty-minded person comes along and says you look like a fly on a can of garbage, pay him no mind. He probably hasn't got the price of a television set."

To play Marlowe, Goodson and Todman had already chosen Phil Carey, then under contract to Columbia's warlord, Harry Cohn, who surprisingly let him go. Carey recollected the endless days of pre-production: "I had a meeting at the Polo Lounge with Chandler, Goodson, and Todman, and everything was agreed. Chandler wrote the screenplay for the first *Philip Marlowe* pilot, which was set in the 1940s. It was so confusing that it had to be rewritten.

"It was only a half-hour show and he was writing almost a novel's worth. We did another pilot, set in the present, and they put a scar on my cheek. That one seemed to work. Mark Goodson told me that Chandler wanted to sit down with me and see how much I knew about Marlowe. So they gave me his novels and I read them. When I'd done that, he asked me about little details in the books, what I thought of some of the people who had played Marlowe in films, and what would I do differently in the television series. It was like being at school. Then he'd ask me about television. Would it be beneficial to him, would he be proud? I told him it was a very limited medium and that it would be difficult to include all his characters in a half-hour. He wasn't very coherent, but he liked the way I looked.

"He was rather crusty and not a very nice man to be around. You could like him, but you wouldn't want to be around him. I did a promotional tour with him; we went on television around the country announcing the program. He didn't like television, but he liked the money it would bring him and he was going to receive money from every *Philip Marlowe* show we did, regardless of whether the writers stole things from his books or wrote original stuff. The network was just using him, really, but as long as he felt some involvement, he didn't mind.

"The show was sponsored by Ted Bates, the agency that represented Viceroy cigarettes and another brand called Life, which had a white tip. As a result of that, the network wouldn't allow the heavy to smoke a cigarette with a white tip. If he smoked, he would have

James Garner, an insufficiently crumpled Marlowe, surveys the first ice-pick: **Marlowe** (1969).

to smoke cigarettes with a brown filter. So if the villain smoked, you could always identify him."

Apart from its brown-filter felons, there was nothing much to distinguish *Philip Marlowe* from its counterparts of the time—*Peter Gunn, Johnny Staccato*, and *77 Sunset Strip*, all of which had better theme tunes, an important consideration for a television series planning a long run. Marlowe's idiosyncrasies included having an apartment overlooking the harbor at Newport Beach and a cabin cruiser to assist in the occasional maritime investigation. Twenty-six episodes were filmed—employing such directors as Irvin Kershner, Arthur Hill, and, on a more regular basis, Gene Wong—then sold by NBC to ABC, which broadcast the first, "The Ugly Duckling," on October 6, 1959, and the last, "You Kill Me," on March 29, 1960. Chandler, who died in La Jolla on March 26, 1959, did not see any of them.

Flash-forward to 1967 in Los Angeles, where independent producers Gabriel Katzka and Sidney Beckerman decided to make a movie based on Chandler's fifth novel, *The Little Sister*, the one he had put aside to write the ill-fated *Playback* screenplay. While trying to finish the book in the summer of 1948, he outlined his difficulties to Hamish Hamilton: "The trouble with the Marlowe character is that he has been written and talked about too much. He's getting self-conscious, trying to live up to his reputation among the quasi-intellectuals. The boy is bothered. He used to be able to spit and throw the ball hard and talk out of the corner of his mouth." About the book itself, he added: "There is nothing in it but style and dialogue and characters. The plot creaks like a broken shutter in an October wind."

The Little Sister was Chandler's first novel for five years—"The only book of mine I have actively disliked," he told the critic James Sandoe. "It was written in a bad mood and I think that comes through." The setting is Hollywood. Marlowe has increased his rate by fifteen dollars to forty dollars a day plus expenses, and the film world provides the moneyed backdrop against which Chandler plays off his reproachful recollections of a world in which he was never at ease. When he describes the agent Sheridan Ballou pacing around his office swinging a Malacca cane ("that an apparently sane man could walk up and down inside the house with a Piccadilly stroll and a monkey stick in his hand"), one remembers Billy Wilder and Chandler's list of complaints about him during the writing of *Double Indemnity.*

Chandler's unyielding antipathy toward Hollywood is complemented by Marlowe's growing sourness toward himself: "I killed my cigarette and got another one out and went through all the slow, futile, face-saving motions of lighting it, getting rid of the match, blowing smoke off to one side, inhaling deeply as though the scrubby little office was a hilltop overlooking the bouncing ocean—all the tired clichéd mannerisms of my trade."

By now it is apparent that neither Chandler nor his mouthpiece Marlowe (ambivalent as their response had always been) liked Los Angeles at all, although the poetic vigor of the descriptive passages might persuade one that this was not the case: "I drove east on Sunset but I didn't go home. At La Brea I turned north and swung over to Highland, out over Cahuenga Pass and down onto Ventura Boulevard, past Studio City and Sherman Oaks and Encino. There was nothing lonely about the trip. There never is on that road. Fast boys in stripped-down Fords shot in and out of the traffic streams, missing fenders by a sixteenth of an inch, but somehow always missing them. Tired men in dusty coupes and sedans winced and tightened their grip on the wheel and ploughed on north and west toward home and dinner, an evening with the sports page, the blatting of the radio, the whining of their spoiled children, and the gabble of their silly wives. I drove on past the gaudy neons and the false fronts behind them, the sleazy hamburger joints that look like palaces under the colors, the circular drive-ins as gay as circuses with the chipper, hard-eyed carhops, the brilliant counters, and the sweaty, greasy kitchens that would have poisoned a toad. Great double trucks rumbled down over Sepulveda from Wilmington and San Pedro and crossed toward the Ridge Route, starting up in low from the traffic lights with a growl of lions in the zoo."

Los Angeles policemen like French and Beyfus are tough but honest. Bay City cops like Moses Maglashan—who wears a pigskin glove on his right hand when questioning suspects—are merely sadistic and corrupt. "What makes you Bay City cops so tough?" French asks him at one point. "You pickle your nuts in salt water or something?" One can tell that French and Beyfus are full of endearing human frailty when they engage in an undignified scrap in front of Marlowe. "It's a new kind of third degree," observes Beyfus ruefully. "The cops beat the hell out of each other and the suspect cracks up from the agony of watching" (a line Stirling Silliphant appropriated unabridged for his screenplay).

The Little Sister was one of the finest novels about Los Angeles published at the time, and Silliphant—whom Beckerman and Katzka had contracted to write the script—wanted to turn it into the definitive Los Angeles movie. When he began work on it, Silliphant had just won an Academy Award for his *In the Heat of the Night* (1967) screenplay. The fact that this put him in considerable demand did not dissuade him from approaching the project the way he did everything else: legwork.

"The script was written after two weeks of going all over town on my own," he said. "Then the director and location people would follow and decide whether or not they wanted to use the places I had chosen. My whole background as a writer lies in that kind of approach. I did a show on CBS television for four years called *Route 66*, which was shot all over the U.S. For every script I was to write, I went to the city in question without even knowing what the story was going to be. Then by walking around and looking at things, the locations and the people suggested the story. So for *The Little Sister* I went around Los Angeles finding the places that I felt would remind one of the Forties and yet be the Sixties. For instance, the Bradbury Building had been used before in several films, but I felt it had such validity as a place to put Marlowe's office that I went ahead. We used Venice as well, for the hotel where Marlowe goes looking for Orrin Quest at the beginning. At the time, if you were looking for any activist, militant, or underground organization, you'd start in Venice. Because even if they aren't there, there are people there who know where they are."

In Chandler's novel, another would-be blackmailer gets an ice-pick through the neck at the Van Nuys Hotel, now called the Barclay, at 4th and Main . . .

Silliphant also set a scene in downtown's sublime Union Station and capitalized on the seedy splendor of the Hotel Alvarado, built in the Twenties on the northeast corner of MacArthur Park, for the flophouse in which the toupeed, would-be blackmailer Hicks gets an ice-pick

. . . in **Marlowe**, the scene is transfered to the Hotel Alvarado, on the northeast corner of MacArthur Park . . .

. . . where Hicks (Jackie Coogan) will soon lose more than his toupee.

through his neck. (In the novel this occurs in the Van Nuys Hotel, now called the Barclay and still flaunting its deteriorating turn-of-century charms near the Bradbury Building at 4th and Main.)

There were reasons other than professional predisposition behind Silliphant's wish to capture Chandler's mood as accurately as possible. As well as knowing his books sufficiently well to recite passages at random, Silliphant had met him on several occasions when he lived in San Diego and Chandler was in neighboring La Jolla. Like most people who had read Chandler's books, Silliphant admired his achievement. Unlike the Hollywood crowd, he also liked him personally.

Clearly, though, changes would have to be made. Much of the dialogue, though still compelling, had become mannered and anachronistic, so Silliphant attempted to find its contemporary equivalent, to invent a style Chandler might have employed had he been writing in the late Sixties. (Not always successfully—Chandler would never have used terms like "a no-no" or "you're something else," which are from somewhere in the hippie twilight zone.)

The film background is shifted to television, by far the more dominant medium of the period, when motion pictures were in decline and the studios had become little more than banks that made deals with independent producers. Accordingly, Mavis Wald (changed, inexplicably, from Mavis Weld) is no longer a starlet but the leading actress in a successful family-viewing television series, making the prospect of unsavory publicity all the more perturbing for the people around her.

Additionally, Silliphant eliminates various inconvenient subplots (more blackmail, a dead gangster), a couple of bitchy actors, a nasty policeman (Maglashan), a film mogul (Jules Oppenheimer, a character purportedly inspired by Y. Frank Freeman, Paramount's West Coast head of production in the Forties), and the pair of cartoon heavies who visit Marlowe in his office and, with the inevitability of another sunrise, offer him money to stay off the case.

To replace the latter, so devalued by television in the intervening years, he brought in Bruce Lee: "I had personal reasons. Bruce was my closest friend and I was studying with him. He was fighting to be recognized as an actor. The industry just didn't seem to hire Asians, didn't even recognize that we have an Asian population here. It's almost as if they didn't *see* those people. Having got Bruce, it seemed appropriate to introduce the martial-arts aspect." Other re-inforcements include a gay hairdresser with premises next door to Marlowe's office and a regular girlfriend called Julie: "It always troubled me in the books that I didn't know where Marlowe was sleeping, although at the time Chandler wrote them I don't suppose it was that important."

The first draft of the screenplay was submitted by Silliphant at the end of June 1967. On July 6, Russell Thatcher, MGM's executive story editor, sent a note to Gabriel Katzka. "Undoubtedly, you have other points that trouble you," reads the final paragraph, "but what seems apparent is that Silliphant has tried to be a bit too fancy for his own good. As you point out, however, this is the first draft, and I don't feel you are in any real trouble." By July 24, the Production Code administration department had applied its collective attention and reported its findings to the studio: "Basically, the material would be acceptable. However, there are certain elements in this present version that would be unacceptable. In the main, these items have to do with various degrees of undress all the way to complete nudity. We direct specific scenes to your attention. P.3: 'He passes a girl with absolutely no stitch of clothing on her.' This of course would be unacceptable under the code. P.44: The expression 'sonofabitch' would not be acceptable. P.45: Mavis's costume as described in scene 140 should not be such as to draw vulgar attention to her semi-nudity. P.121: The expression 'goddamn' is unacceptable. As you know, our final judgement will be based on the finished picture."

Evidently, then, Silliphant wanted to make a tough, contemporary Marlowe movie, one that the Production Code people would no doubt refer to as "unacceptable." Enter the director, Paul Bogart, with the intention of making it restrained and purist. Bogart, a veteran TV director and the winner of two Emmy Awards, was making his first feature film. Like James Garner, who was set to play Marlowe, he had been unsettled by the assassinations of Martin Luther King and Robert Kennedy, which preceded the beginning of filming in 1968. Consequently, he wanted to minimize the bloodshed. "There's very little violence in it," he reflected with some pride. "There are ice-picks in the neck, but those were done in the style of 'movie murders,' and the one time Marlowe is beaten up, you see it mainly through car windows. The fact that the picture avoids most direct violence adds to the old-fashioned Forties feeling I wanted to convey.

"I read the script first, then the novel. The script was a disappointment to me because, while I wanted to do a traditional Chandler mystery, Stirling had made awkward attempts to bring it up to date. There were hippies, which I tried to cut down as much as I could. They're there at the beginning, but I cut a whole sequence in a disco, which made everybody happy because it meant money saved. I had tried at first to persuade the producers to do it in period, but they said no because automobiles and costumes would have added to the cost of the picture. The producers had definite ideas, not many of which I agreed with." More significantly, he did not agree on much with Stirling Silliphant.

"The fact that Jim Garner and Paul Bogart had such strong feelings against violence," said Silliphant, "creates a difficult problem when you're dealing with a Philip Marlowe story. You have to find bodies, get beaten up, shoot people, and hack your way around Los Angeles. So when the heavies rough up Marlowe outside Mavis's apartment, I wanted it to have the power of the scene at the end of

Steelgrave's heavies apply the treatment. Marlowe takes it all in the stomach.

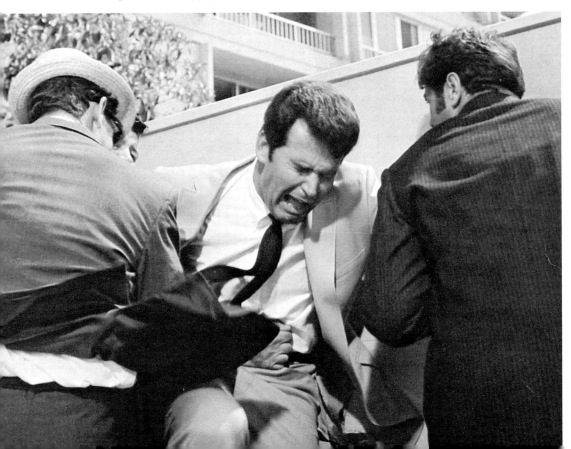

On the Waterfront, whereas it came out extremely superficial—it had no persuasiveness at all. The film did not have a violent attitude. A lot of the vigor, anger, and cynicism had been eroded. I felt Bogart's direction was too romantic, too pastel, and Garner chose to interpret it in a manner that worked for him but wasn't what I had hoped. He's a marvelous actor and he has some very good scenes. I just wish he had been a bit shabbier, a bit less *nice*.

"If I hadn't cared so much about Chandler, it wouldn't have mattered. But I thought *The Little Sister* was one of his best books and I didn't want anyone to screw it up, starting with myself. So the only changes I made were for reasons of audience attitude in the Sixties, and that was a personal judgement. Toward the end, when they're at Steelgrave's house on Mount Wilson, I wrote one of the toughest, deadliest scenes of shooting and savagery you could imagine. Both Garner and Bogart were horrified—they told me I'd set the country back a decade and refused to do it. Jimmy wouldn't act in it. Paul wouldn't shoot it."

Marlowe and Mavis (Gayle Hunnicutt) at Steelgrave's house on Mount Wilson.

While conceding that he wanted to make a more fundamentally orthodox detective thriller than Silliphant, Bogart denied any attempt to bowdlerize the steely disenchantment of Chandler's mood: "I tried to do what the book told me. I believe I'm an instrument of the writer. If anything, I was interested in Marlowe being less chipper and bright, more tired and threadbare. I had to stop people from cleaning his car every time we were going to do a shot. I had a cameraman who was one of the greats of Hollywood—William H. Daniels, who used to be Garbo's cameraman. He was a gentleman, but he was the wrong man for the picture. I wanted somebody looser, faster, and less careful. He lit everything painfully, especially the women. He was afraid of shooting the face of a live television screen for fear of what the quality might be like. We had fights about that."

The impression nevertheless is of some unsanctified mating of *Pillow Talk* and *The Moving Target*: insistently frothy, self-consciously Chandlerian. Over an elaborately geometric title sequence—in which Mavis (Gayle Hunnicutt) engages in rose-tinted heavy-petting around a swimming pool with her racketeer lover Steelgrave (H.M. Wynant) while being photographed by someone later revealed to be her own

The heavy petting that begins the blackmail: Mavis and her racketeer lover Steelgrave (H.M. Wynant).

brother Orrin—the familiar theme song, tyrannically inbred in Sixties movies, invades the soundtrack with all the diffidence of an early party arrival with a string of fairy lights around its neck. "If I could reach your mind, little sister/If I could get inside your mind," goes the song, voicing one of the modish preoccupations of its period. (Bogart was less than entirely satisfied with the visual aspects of all this: "The steamy lovemaking of which Orrin was taking pictures was so lost that it was hard to see what he could possibly be using as blackmail.")

The song continues on Marlowe's car radio as he drives through the dilapidated beach suburb of Venice looking for Orrin, and reappears intermittently in various instrumental arrangements throughout the film, once accompanying a television dance routine, later a striptease show. In this respect, it predates *The Long Goodbye,* which applies the same musical principle in a more ironic and fully realized manner.

The first glimpse of James Garner at the wheel confirms all of one's preemptive reservations about his appropriateness for the role. He has a suntan for a start. Marlowe would have a suntan only if he had been tied to a stake in the middle of the Mojave desert preapplied with factor 15. Marlowe, now charging a hundred dollars a day plus expenses, should have a slightly forbidding air about him that discourages people from taking liberties. Garner looks as if he would invite them to kick sand in his face. He is insufficiently crumpled and excessively well-groomed, too intrinsically lightweight as a presence and as a personality to play the role with any conviction. Garner is engaging enough—indeed, this is a creditable representation of his own typical performance, full of the wry details that go to make it up—but his involvement in *Marlowe* makes it appear like nothing more than a dry run for *The Rockford Files,* which a few years later would tread similar territory more effectively as a television series about a private detective.

In fact, much of the film *looks* like a TV pilot, despite its attractive color photography and extensive location work. Most of the problems, claimed Bogart, arose at the editing stage: "The picture was trampled on. The plot and continuity were brutalized. I tried to rescue as much as I could of the feeling that had been intended. In the opening scene, when Marlowe drives through Venice, there was a whole lot of atmosphere: oil derricks right outside someone's living room, bicycles, joggers, weary people flopped on the beach. That all went. It was cut by Gene Ruggiero, who was terrified of the head Metro cutter, Margaret Booth, and slavishly obeyed her, even when he had misunderstood her instructions, which were often in contradiction of mine.

"For example, that scene in which Bruce Lee and Garner are on the rooftop was done with a concealed trampoline so that Bruce could jump, come up with his feet first, and sail off the building. I edited it so that it worked perfectly, then came in a few days later and looked at the scene and it no longer convinced me. I said, 'Wait a minute, you've changed that cut,' and Ruggiero said he had to because Miss Booth had told him to. It was finally restored, but after I left the picture, there were other changes made that made my heart bleed and made no sense of the action. In Rita Moreno's strip dance at the end, they cut part of a scene where Marlowe is leaving. She watches

Marlowe and Wong (Bruce Lee) in combat. The latter will soon be flying toward the city lights.

him go, makes some mildly obscene gesture to him, and exposes her bosom. They cut that. It made no sense. First of all, she was wearing a false chest that the Metro costume department had built. Secondly, it *was* 1969, Rita's exposure was relatively temperate, and the whole business mattered in her relationship with Marlowe."

The spring cleaning, however, is not confined to editing but extends to the principal characters. Mavis becomes a sympathetic victim who can barely hold her halo straight as a result of the pressures, while Dolores (an apt if obvious part for Rita Moreno) is a frisky stripper rather than a nasty nymphomaniac, although she does remain a murderer. Only Orfamay, who set the whole mess in motion, comes close to Chandler's representation of her in Sharon Farrell's plain-frocked, bogus-innocent, mean-spirited portrayal.

The peripheral figures, particularly the created ones, are more consistently interesting. Bruce Lee, in the scene where he isn't jumping off the top of a tall building, destroys Marlowe's office in two balletically lethal stages. As his introductory salvo, he kicks in the wall and decapitates a hatstand. Then, after Marlowe has resisted Steelgrave's offer of hush money ("Tell him you met the last of a dying dynasty. King of the fools. Unassailably virtuous. Invariably broke," writes Silliphant in one of his few lapses into precisely the stilted qualities of Chandler's dialogue that he sought to avoid), the demolition is completed when Lee eliminates the chandelier, door, and desk with a single protracted movement. Finally, after a seamless pause, he puts on his shades with a flourish and leaves the room.

William Daniels (minus the cinematographer's middle initial), then the most accomplished character actor in Hollywood when playing neurotically punctilious middle-Americans, is less devastating but comparably twitchy playing Crowell, Mavis's agent, now turned into a partner in the advertising agency representing her show's sponsor. His brief sequence of scenes with Garner is one of the real pleasures of the film. At one point they are in a television control room watching the run-through of a new program when Marlowe spots Greta Garbo emoting her way through *Grand Hotel* on an adjacent black-and-white monitor. "She was great, wasn't she?" he observes fondly. "The show we're doing," replies Daniels with suppressed irritation, "is over there." Continuing their discussion in the back of his chauffeured car on the way to the airport, Daniels informs him that Mavis has the leading part in "the top-rated sitcom in the country." Marlowe

Orfamay (Sharon Farrell) attacks Mavis.

fails to return the correct signals of recognition within the required second. "Situation comedy," he adds.

Equally effective are the details that enliven what might otherwise be routine set-pieces. Marlowe's conversation with Orfamay at the snack counter in Union Station is conducted while a woman, unwittingly caught between them, tries not to register alarm as the details of Orrin's death become more explicit. When Lagardie dies after shooting Dolores and himself at the strip club, his fingernails scrape down the backstage blackboard. (Lagardie, too, has changed from his original incarnation. In the novel, he is more like Amthor in *Farewell, My Lovely*: a legitimate dope peddler to the rich needle classes.)

Reflecting the vogue in detective thrillers for single-name titles, pioneered in the U.S. by *Harper* (although not in Britain, where *Harper* was changed back to *The Moving Target*), *The Little Sister* became *Marlowe* in April 1969, six months before its release. When it finally emerged, the *New York Times*, to Bogart's delight, called it "the most promising sleeper of 1946." Most of the other American critics were not so enthusiastic—indeed, Nat Freedland of *Entertainment World* suggested some special penalty be imposed on anyone making a routine film from a Chandler novel—but their British counterparts applauded its unpretentious popcorn value.

Stirling Silliphant also wrote a screenplay of *The Long Goodbye* for the same producers, Katzka and Beckerman. "It was a very difficult script to do because it's a tough story. It goes on and on; you think it's ending, then there's another ending. Sidney and Gabe weren't encouraged by the returns on *Marlowe,* so it never went into production. At some point, they either sold the rights or their option lapsed." *The Long Goodbye* seemed destined for a long life on a dusty shelf.

Just three years later, it climbed down.

"THE LONG GOODBYE"

CHAPTER 12

RIP VAN MARLOWE

The Long Goodbye

If Marlowe had surrendered to the occasional moment of self-doubt in *The Little Sister*, by 1951, when Chandler began to write his sixth novel around the character, he was practically corroded by uncertainty. "If being in revolt against a corrupt society constitutes being immature," Chandler wrote of him that year, "then Philip Marlowe is extremely immature. If seeing dirt where there is dirt constitutes an inadequate social adjustment, then Philip Marlowe has inadequate social adjustment. Of course, Marlowe is a failure and he knows it. He is a failure because he hasn't any money. A man who without physical handicaps cannot make a decent living is always a failure and usually a moral failure. But a lot of very good men have been failures because their particular talents did not suit their time and place."

The essence of Marlowe's problem, of course, lays with his creator. When Chandler wrote *The Long Good Bye* (the novel's title is hyphenated), he was dutifully sober but habitually depressed, a sense of worthy industriousness having been drafted in to supplant the well-oiled fluency. With no private life beyond whatever comfort he could give to a wife who was dying slowly and painfully of fibrosis, he surrendered everything to the accomplishment of his longest and most ambitious novel.

Impressive as it turned out to be—it is the most enduring of his books by far, as well as the most labyrinthine—one can sense the weariness: a dispirited man of sixty-three chronicling the decline of a private detective who, although some twenty years younger, was aging with the same intensity as his begetter. For Marlowe, the days of spending most of his waking hours upholding righteousness from his squalid office on Hollywood Boulevard are over. Now he lives in a hillside house in Laurel Canyon, across from a eucalyptus grove. He is kind to drunks and responsive to attractive women for reasons other than the eliciting of information. He thinks too much.

Despite this, it is evident from the first page alone that none of Chandler's aphoristic flourishes will be absent. "He was still holding the door open," Chandler wrote, "because Terry Lennox's left foot was still dangling outside, as if he had forgotten he had one." A few paragraphs later, "the girl gave him a look that ought to have stuck at least four inches out of his back."

When Chandler sent the 92,000-word draft to his agent, Bernice Baumgarten, in 1952, he stressed that he was relatively unconcerned about the mystery itself, "but I cared about the people, about this strange corrupt world we live in, and how any man who tried to be honest looks in the end either sentimental or plain foolish."

The novel's original title, one it re-acquired intermittently during revision, was *Summer in Idle Valley*, although it had returned to being *The Long Good-Bye* by the time of its publication in 1953. Intimidated by its length and complexity, the movie world kept its distance for twelve years until, in October 1965, an item appeared in *Variety* reporting that the novel had been acquired by Gershwin-Kastner Productions for filming at the Warner studios in Burbank and on location. More than two years later, in February 1968, a story in the *Hollywood Reporter* announced that Stirling Silliphant had begun work on an adaptation of the book for MGM and Katzka-Berne Productions, the team that was already preparing to make his script of *The Little Sister*. By 1972 the project was back with Kastner again, this time in association with United Artists, neither of whose favored directors, Howard Hawks and Peter Bogdanovich, were available. It was finally offered to Brian Hutton, who had recently enjoyed grand slams at the box office with *Where Eagles Dare* (1968) and *Kelly's Heroes* (1970). The fact that neither picture had anything to do with detectives was considered an asset.

Elliott Gould as Philip Marlowe: a figure of the past adrift in the present in a city spinning toward the future in **The Long Goodbye** (1973).

Silliphant's screenplay, in consonance with his approach to *The Little Sister*, had been largely faithful to the novel in that it updated rather than overhauled the narrative. Indeed, the most radical modification he made was to amalgamate the characters of Linda Loring and Eileen Wade into one called Linda Wade. Hutton, on the other hand, wanted to turn the whole thing on its head.

Leigh Brackett, whose work in the movies since *The Big Sleep* had been confined almost entirely to Howard Hawks pictures, was hired to write the new script. Her problems were considerable, and it was not just a question of length. "Structurally, the book is awkward," she wrote in *Take One* magazine. "Chandler is in effect telling two stories . . . the two hung together by an involved and tortuous chain of coincidences. While the same criticism can be leveled against *The Big Sleep* as well, there is a difference. In *Sleep,* the stories are better integrated, and Chandler never gives the reader time to consider the holes in the connective tissue. In *Good-Bye* he gives far too much time . . .

"Technically, the books differ greatly. *Sleep* is brisk and extroverted, a succession of cinematic scenes. Marlowe's stream of consciousness is manageable, easily translatable into dialogue. *Good-Bye* is endlessly introspective, with long passages of subjective philosophical comment that are impossible to translate . . . There is nothing wrong with this at all. Chandler wasn't trying to do *The Big Sleep* over again. He was doing something quite different, making a different set of comments of life and truth and love and friendship. But what a reader will hold still for, savor, and enjoy on the printed page is one thing. Putting it into visual form is quite another."

Brackett began by trying to incorporate as much as possible of Chandler's own language and attitude. After a while, it became clear that it wasn't working: "Everything that was fresh and exciting about Philip Marlowe in the Forties had become a cliché, outworn by imitation and overuse. The tough loner with the sardonic tongue and the cast-iron gut had become a caricature . . . Time had removed the context. The Los Angeles upon which Chandler based his literary work is as dead as Babylon. The characters with which he peopled it were never drawn from life anyway, but from the films of the Twenties and Thirties: shadow-play hoods and gamblers, madcap heiresses, and tough cops. They don't make movies like that anymore. We don't speak that language anymore. We've got a whole new generation and a whole new bag of clichés—just as phony but different."

By the end of the first draft, Brackett, encouraged by Brian Hutton, had reached at least one conclusion: "Terry Lennox had become a clear-cut villain, and it seemed that the only satisfactory ending was for the cruelly diddled Marlowe to blow Terry's guts out, partly to keep Terry from getting away with it all, partly out of sheer human rage." Consequently, the issue of whether Marlowe would or would not have shot a friend becomes irrelevant. In the novel, Lennox is merely deceitful. In the film, he is homicidally deceitful, while Eileen, once a double murderer, becomes little more than a confused adulterer.

With various problems delaying production, and the resultant loss of Hutton to another film, Brackett used the time to take a machete to the script, compressing the narrative, dropping half the characters (Sewell Endicott, Howard Spencer, Linda Loring, Harlan Potter, Bernie Ohls), moulding Menendez into Marty Augustine, and giving sharper definition to the new conception of Marlowe. The arrival of Robert Altman as director—his acceptance prompted mainly by the fact that a United Artists executive wanted Elliott Gould to play Marlowe—added the likelihood of pissing on the altar to an expanding catalogue of desecration.

From then on, it became even more probable that Marlowe would be presented as a slobbish, gullible anachronism—a projection, Altman felt, of the way Chandler might have viewed the world in 1972. "I see Marlowe the way Chandler saw him," he told Brackett, "a loser. But a real loser, not the fake winner that Chandler made out of him. A loser all the way."

Terry Lennox (Jim Bouton): part of the new border-line-criminal Southern Californian bogus elite.

Since *M*A*S*H* had established his and Altman's careers in 1970, Gould—as well as having the distinction of appearing in one of Ingmar Bergman's most unremittingly tedious films, *The Touch*—had suffered a series of commercial catastrophes and had been in dispute with Warner Bros. While making *A Glimpse of Tiger* for them—never completed and, the story goes, recycled the following year as *What's Up Doc?* with Gould's ex-wife Barbra Streisand in the part originally intended for him—Gould was reported to have intimidated his leading lady, Kim Darby, brawled with director Anthony Harvey, and engaged in such boisterously temperamental behavior that the company collected on an insurance policy claiming he was insane. Gould denied all charges but agreed to pay the production costs to date. While United Artists understandably required some kind of psychiatric test before going ahead with casting him in *The Long Goodbye*, Altman could see no one else as Marlowe.

Next he had to find his Eileen Wade. Gould himself favored Jennifer O'Neill but Altman had other ideas. At the end of 1971, McGraw-Hill had announced the publication of Howard Hughes' memoirs to be written by little-known novelist Clifford Irving, whose most recent book *Fake!* was a study of the famous art forger Elmyr de Hory. Just more than three months later, McGraw-Hill and *Life*, who had bought the serial rights, admitted they had been hoaxed: a fake biography by a faker's biographer. Consequently, Irving, who had evidently taken more than notes when interviewing de Hory, enjoyed a kind of attention he could never have contemplated when making his plans in Ibiza, an island colonized by dreamers and schemers. One of the witnesses in his trial, a Danish baroness named Nina van Pallandt—who had sung in a folk duo with her husband Frederick until their separation in 1969—received almost equal prominence as a consequence of a four-day romantic interlude with him in Mexico, where he was concluding a few details in his elaborate swindle.

"I felt like a total freak," she said. "I spent one weekend with Irving, the first time in my life I went on a weekend with someone I wasn't married to. It hadn't even seemed important at the time. Suddenly I had offers of concert tours, promotional T-shirts with Howard Hughes' picture on them; you can imagine. Notoriety is viewed very differently in America from the way it is in Europe. In Europe, it is a scandal to be associated with a crook; in America it's terrific and you get your name in the papers."

Despite her distaste for the events that followed, van Pallandt's career benefited greatly from them, particularly on television, where Dick Cavett, Mike Douglas, David Frost, and Johnny Carson regularly invited her onto their shows. Altman saw her on Carson's and telephoned her manager, who, unaware of who Altman was, did not return the call. Van Pallandt herself saw his name on a notepad and rang the number. When she arrived at the Sherry Netherlands Hotel in New York, where Altman was staying, she nearly collided with Lauren Hutton, who had arrived at the same time for the same role.

"It became apparent that United Artists didn't want me," said van Pallandt, "because of my notoriety and because they thought I couldn't act. Bob asked them to do a screen test, which they wouldn't do, so I paid for my own. I think he found it intriguing to cast me in that part—you know, the mysterious lady with the shady side to her. He certainly fought to get me."

He got her, as *Variety* would announce with its customary flourish: "Nina van Pallandt, Swedish nitery thrush who zoomed to prominence because of her association with alleged hoaxer Clifford Irving, has been tapped to co-star with Elliott Gould in UA's *The Long Goodbye.*"

Having found his Eileen Wade in a Danish nitery thrush—*Variety* clearly put all its Scandinavians in the same sauna—Altman continued with the rest of his casting, which was to comprise his characteristic blend of willful spontaneity and adventurous eccentricity. Dan Blocker, originally set to play Roger Wade, died before filming began (earning a posthumous dedication), and Sterling Hayden, looking as if he were in rehearsal for a remake of *The Old Man and the Sea*, took the role to pay for a bathroom on his houseboat. Mark Rydell, a former actor turned director, was persuaded back in front of the cameras to play Marty Augustine, and Jo Ann Brody, whom Altman wrote into the film as Augustine's girlfriend, was a waitress at a restaurant in Malibu called The Raft, where he and Rydell had a discussion over dinner one evening.

Two real estate women doing the inventory of the Wade home toward the end of the film are Miss Brody's mother and a friend, both on a brief visit from Oklahoma City. David Carradine has a one-minute cameo as Marlowe's garrulous hippie cellmate; former baseball star Jim Bouton plays Terry Lennox; Henry Gibson, still synonymous with

Laugh-In, is Dr. Verringer; and Altman's janitor, Rodney Moss, has his moment of fame as a supermarket attendant. Add to that a discredited leading man with insurance problems, a Danish baroness concerned about her notoriety, and an old sea-dog trying to afford a bathroom, and one can only conclude that Altman's appetite for risk persistently eclipses his regard for safety.

It was indicative of Altman's objective that the reading material he gave his cast was not Chandler's novel but *Raymond Chandler Speaking*, a collection of his letters and essays. Altman was less concerned with making a film about Philip Marlowe than one about Raymond Chandler, with Gould and Hayden representing different aspects of his character. *The Long Goodbye* itself simply provided a convenient canvas upon which to trace new elements.

In Altman's films of the Seventies—both the glowing, elegiac portraits of people in a particular landscape and period like *McCabe and Mrs. Miller* (1971) and *Thieves Like Us* (1973), and the intricate mosaics of collisions and collusions such as *Nashville* (1975) and *A Wedding* (1978)—conversation is treated as overlapping blocks of sound. When several people are speaking at once, as they often do in his movies, the result merges with whatever background sounds might accompany it. Significant conversations are permitted to compete for attention with insignificant ones and along with all the other audio elements. What matters gets through.

Altman wanted the film to have a surreal, pastel quality, like a creamy, dreamy recollection of the 1950s, to contrast with the tawdry opportunism of the contemporary Los Angeles he wished to portray. His cinematographer, Vilmos Zsigmond, applied a technique called post-flashing, which, through a complex process of light exposure, would soften colors in a way that suggested some half-remembered reverie.

Altman also encouraged his actors to develop their parts themselves, resulting in a style that often suggests improvisation. Pauline Kael, an admirer of Altman, described *Brewster McCloud* (1971) as "like a rehearsal, with the actors just saying anything while waiting for the script to turn up." Altman claimed to director Robert Benton that his films were not improvised; he simply preferred to write the final dialogue for the day's shooting early on the same morning. "It's just a technique," he explained, "for keeping the working process as spontaneous as possible." He emphasized that only the drinking scene between Gould and Hayden was improvised in *The Long Goodbye*, although van Pallandt recalled that ad-libbing was also required in the unconvincing episode in which she and Gould talk to the police after Hayden's drowning—"We were just told what to convey."

Van Pallandt was also struck by Altman's regard for detail. On two occasions in the movie she offers Gould a dried apricot (the first time he accepts but puts it in his top pocket; the second he refuses on the grounds that they give him diarrhea): "The apricot thing was invented because Bob asked me what I wanted around me that made me feel comfortable. I said cigarettes and dried apricots. In the film I couldn't have the cigarettes—Elliott, who didn't smoke at the time while all the rest of us did, was the only one allowed cigarettes—so I had the dried apricots. Bob also put a picture of Leonard Cohen in my bedroom. Cohen had done the songs for *McCabe and Mrs. Miller* and I used to do his song 'Bird on a Wire' in my cabaret show, so we had discussed him. With Altman, nothing is incidental."

The Long Goodbye is a film in which a figure of the past is adrift in the present in a city spinning toward the future. It begins with a brief burst of "Hooray for Hollywood," one of the numbers from Busby Berkeley's *Hollywood Hotel* (1937), in which Dick Powell had appeared before the allure of dramatic acting and playing Philip Marlowe became irresistible.

This immediately establishes a tone of irony in a film populated by people who still believe implicitly in movie mythology. The guard at the entrance to the Malibu Colony treats visitors to his impressions of Barbara Stanwyck, James Stewart, Cary Grant, and Walter Brennan, almost as a condition of letting them through the gate. Marlowe refers to both *The Invisible Man* ("I've seen all your pictures, too," he says to a man in the hospital whose head is entirely covered by bandages) and *The Thin Man* ("Come on, Asta, I'm honking my horn, you're supposed to get out of the way," he admonishes a dog crossing the road in front of his car.) Some characters, like Roger Wade, employ it as the departure point for some celluloid idea of themselves—in his case, playing out the drunken writer role as far as he can take it. For others, such as Terry Lennox and Marty Augustine, it provides a backdrop of rationalization for their showy villainy. Even Augustine's henchmen view the world in terms of its connections with the films they know. In the scene where he threatens Marlowe with castration, he instructs them all to take their clothes off, except for a

Marlowe's apartment building on Hightower Drive, with the elevator inside the tower.

Mexican with body scars, who is permitted to leave the room. "George Raft never took his clothes off," one of them complains. (Another strips to reveal a familiarly large torso below an unfamiliarly small moustache. It is a silent, unbilled Arnold Schwarzenegger at the start of his movie career.)

The opening glimpse of Marlowe establishes that, however he develops in the course of the picture, he will have little in common with Humphrey Bogart. He is the most unheroic of sights, lying on a bed fully clothed, asleep with the lights on. A cat crawls across his chest and wakes him. He looks at his watch, scratches his head, and lights a cigarette. While the rest of California worries about its health, he chain-smokes untipped Camels—striking the match on the nearest available surface—talks to his cat and himself, and will be seen in the same clothes (dark suit and tie, white shirt) throughout the film. He drives a 1948 Lincoln Continental (license plate PVT EYE), charges fifty dollars a day plus expenses (half the rate demanded by James Garner in _Marlowe_ four years earlier), and, like his literary counter-part, does not do divorce work. One concludes without too much prompting that he is a good-natured mess. Even his Spanish is sloppy; his cat door reads El Porto Del Gato, a confusion of definite article, gender, and even language.

Rejected by the cat after trying to serve a dinner of cottage cheese with raw egg ("Can't do better than that at Chasen's," he mumbles as he dishes up), he decides to drive to an all-night supermarket on Lankershim Boulevard to buy some Coury's Brand cat food

The adjacent apartment where his scantily clad neighbors practice their yoga exercises.

(Pussy Delight in Brackett's original script), the only kind his fastidious pet will tolerate. As he leaves his apartment—the prototypal Hollywood period building, on Hightower Drive just off Highland Avenue—he is asked by his neighbors, hippie girls devoted to scantily clad outdoor yoga, to buy them some Brownie Mix with which to make hash cookies. "You're the nicest neighbor we ever had," says their representative. "Got to be the nicest neighbor," Marlowe mutters as he shuffles toward the elevator. "I'm a private eye. It's okay with me."

This is the first time he says, "It's okay with me" and it will not be the last. He says it to the cat when it subsequently refuses its food; to the police as they take him to the station for questioning; to Eileen Wade on the telephone before meeting her; twice at Verringer's clinic; to the Wades together; to Augustine's girlfriend; and to the real-estate women. Mostly he says it to himself. After a while, it becomes difficult to conjecture what is *not* okay with him.

The frequency of this, however, is nothing by comparison with the number of times one hears John Williams' and Johnny Mercer's theme song, which, repeated in numerous wittily disguised variations, punctuates the film. We hear a piano rendition behind Marlowe's efforts to feed his cat; two different vocal versions (by Jack Sheldon and Clydie King), which accompany Lennox and Marlowe as they drive toward their different destinations during the credits; an orchestral Muzak version as Marlowe walks around the supermarket; more piano back at his apartment, this time with added humming; a Spanish-guitar-and-castanets version as he and Lennox approach the Tijuana border at dawn (similar Latin variations will follow: dogs in Mexico have sex to it, Marlowe approaches Lennox's hide-out with the most mournful version of all playing in the background). The pianist in the bar where he collects his messages rehearses it. ("Are you practicing for the hit parade?" asks Marlowe, betraying his antiquated view of the world with a single phrase.) It plays on Marty Augustine's car radio; a jazz variation will accompany Marlowe's pursuit of Eileen Wade's car (licence plates LUV YOU) as he runs down Westwood Boulevard, having just emerged from the 9000 Building on Sunset, several miles away. Even the Wade doorbell plays the first few notes. Still more remarkably, a Mexican band performs it as a funeral march. "The funeral march was printed, bound, and presented to the local band leader in Tepoztlan, which represented Otatoclan in the film," said van Pallandt. "Even to this day, they play 'The Long Goodbye' as a funeral march. We told them it was an American funeral march. They didn't know what they were playing but learned it with great solemnity."

There is no introduction to Marlowe's relationship with Terry Lennox. It is assumed that they know each other well when he arrives at Marlowe's door with his hands and face scratched after, he claims, a fight with his wife. He asks to be driven to Tijuana. In a Los Angeles of all-night supermarkets, stoned hippies, and multi-racial underworld gangs, Lennox in his white suit is part of the new borderline-criminal Southern Californian bogus elite.

When Marlowe returns from Tijuana, the girls are outside doing their exercises and the police are waiting to question him. "Is this the bit where I say 'What is this all about?' and he says, 'Shut up, I ask the questions'?" Marlowe inquires in one of the few lines lifted from the novel, before being taken to the station (the now-closed Lincoln Heights jail in East Los Angeles). During his interrogation, he covers his face with fingerprint ink and does an impression of Al Jolson. Observing behind a one-way window, of which Marlowe is fully aware, are a black policeman and a white lieutenant. The exchange that follows is not in Brackett's script and was probably invented by the playful, mischievous Altman. "He's a real cutie pie, lieutenant," says the black policeman.

Marlowe under interrogation: "It's okay with me."

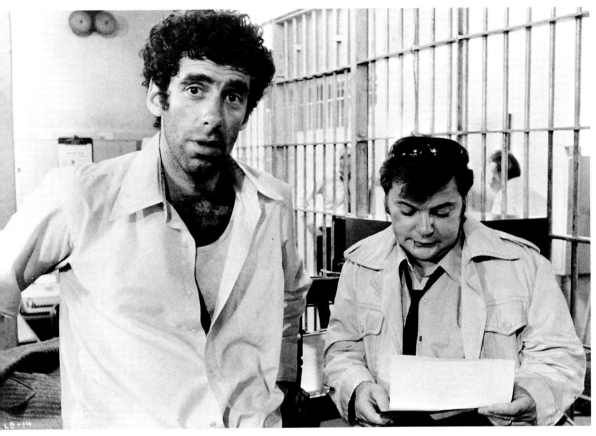

Marlowe: more questions at the police station.

"He's a smart-ass, that's what he is."

"That's what I meant."

"Why don't you learn to say what you mean?"

"He's a real smart-ass, lieutenant."

The lieutenant leaves him to join Marlowe on the other side of the glass. Knowing he is no longer audible, the black policeman discharges his suppressed rage with the vigor one expects of a man who has had to acquiesce too much, too often: "He's the cutie pie, lieutenant. You're the smart-ass, you honky little bastard."

Even allowing for the constant changes made to a script during filming, at this point, only nine pages into the screenplay, hardly anyone has said what was written for them to say. Sometimes it has been improved on, and all kinds of incidental details have been added to the basic speeches and instructions (the exchange between the policemen, for example), but so much has been disregarded or embroidered by Altman that there does not appear to be much point in paying someone of Leigh Brackett's stature to write it in the first place. It could just as easily have been made up, as much of it was.

Several significant scenes in her original screenplay are omitted from the final picture. Some may not even have been filmed: a scene at the Carne Organization, the detective bureau where Marlowe goes to begin trying to track down Roger Wade; his subsequent conversation with Eileen; an exchange in the car with Wade on the way back from Verringer's clinic; a scene at Detective Farmer's office; an additional discussion with Verringer after Wade's death; and, most importantly, a scene in which Eileen Wade is seen to receive the package with Augustine's money from Terry Lennox in Mexico, the first she knows of his whereabouts. Altman, capitalizing on Nina van Pallandt's error in telling Marlowe "I like what you did for my friend"—it should have been "*your* friend"—decided to suggest that she was aware all along.

The best amendment of all is a revised scene dated June 21, 1972. Whether it was revised by Brackett, by Altman, or by committee is not clear. Marty Augustine and his hoods visit Marlowe to try to discover the whereabouts of the considerable sum owed to him by Terry Lennox. Augustine is everything the Seventies racketeer should be: flamboyant, self-regarding, ethnically proud (Jewish and upset at missing Friday night at temple), with a wife at a health farm and three children at summer camps. He calls Marlowe "cheapie" (Wade refers to him as "Marlboro." The sentiment is right, the brand wrong) and, as his subordinates ransack the private eye's apartment, Augustine wants to be sure Marlowe realizes that cheap is what he is not: "You know where I live? In Trousdale, three acres. President Nixon used to live next door. I take tennis lessons three times a week on my own court. I'm in perfect physical shape. Punch me in the stomach as hard as you can."

Mark Rydell is perfect as Augustine, whose affluent delinquency is matched by his explosive viciousness. He is much given to soliloquizing, which he does with the complete attention of his comical accomplices. He has a girlfriend, whom he treats with scrupulous politeness but speaks to in the same way as one might address a small child. "Excuse me," he says to her, explaining that he and the

Marlowe visits Eileen Wade (Nina van Pallandt) . . .

boys are going up to Marlowe's apartment, adding unnecessarily, "You can play the radio if you want" (the theme song is playing again). Eventually, she becomes bored and follows them upstairs. Augustine clearly needs to show Marlowe the kind of gesture of which he is capable. "The single most important person in my life next to my family," he gushes, pointing to her. She has requested a Coca-Cola, but all Marlowe has are some dregs at the bottom of an open bottle, which Augustine suddenly smashes across her face. She is a mess of wounds, her beauty destroyed in a single action. Even the gang is openmouthed in its astonishment. "That's someone I love," says Augustine as his parting shot. "You I don't even like."

Harry, one of Augustine's lackeys, is assigned to tail Marlowe. Greeting him the following morning after successfully giving him the slip the night before, Marlowe is asked by Harry, who is fascinated by the girls in the neighboring apartment, what they do for a living. "They dip candles," Marlowe replies. Harry is both confused and appalled: "I can remember when people just had jobs." Marlowe likes Harry. He flatters him ("Harry, I'm proud to have you following me"). He gives him advice. He hands him the address of where he is going. He even arranges, to Harry's complete bewilderment, for the Malibu Colony guard to do an impression of Walter Brennan for him.

. . . then visits her again.

Sterling Hayden (as Roger Wade) took the role to pay for a bathroom on his houseboat.

The scene with Harry is Brackett filtered through Altman. From then on, the revisions becomes more radical. Altman replaces a wordy and explicit exchange between Marlowe and Wade with a shorter scene involving the latter and Eileen, written by Sterling Hayden himself and even then changed substantially. As they argue, Marlowe patrols the shoreline, reflected in the window, ludicrously over-dressed, his lack of familiarity with the ways of the beach all too evident. Brackett's Marlowe is considerably more assertive toward Wade. "You are a shit, Roger," he informs him. "A real shit. You lean on people, you squash them, you beat them out of shape, you make them lie down and roll over. You can't take no for an answer. I am not going to stay with you. Now why don't you get to your typewriter, rough-hewn country genius? Stop whining and start working." This is a speech that is out of synch with Elliott Gould's interpretation of Marlowe. He would never say these lines, so he doesn't.

Wade's subsequent death scene is all Altman's invention. Where Brackett has him shooting his brains out, and Chandler has Eileen shoot them out for him, Altman gives him an exit worthy of James Mason in *A Star is Born*. As Marlowe and Eileen, believing Wade to be in an alcoholic stupor, chat over Chicken Kiev and wine—soured only by Marlowe's insistence on discussing Marty Augustine's visit to the Wade House—Wade walks into the Pacific with Marlowe, Eileen, and a Doberman in delayed pursuit.

There were three different Dobermans, it seems. "There was one that was fierce, one that was less fierce, and one that went in the water," recalled Nina van Pallandt. "We spent so much time in the water waiting for that dog to come out with the stick. It was endless. My dress got smaller and smaller every time I went in. And it turned out that Elliott doesn't like the water and can't swim. I thought his panic and fury were just good acting, but he was totally freaked out by the whole thing."

And so to Mexico, where Marlowe goes for the final confrontation, with Lennox's postal gift of a $5000 bill as inducement money, successfully proffered as a "charity donation" to the local police chief in a conversation so brazenly post-synched—to avoid upsetting their hosts in Tepoztlan with insinuations of bribery—as to be risible.

Having passed on his cash to the desired effect, Marlowe goes to Lennox's hide-out, where he is lying in a hammock by a stream. A few words are exchanged. Then, with the minimum of ceremony, he shoots him. The image of Lennox floating on the water lingers over that of the tree-lined approach road, along which Eileen Wade is driving her Jeep. The road is deserted, as it was when Marlowe walked up it. They pass one another. She stops briefly, then drives on. Suddenly people begin to appear from all corners as Marlowe plays the harmonica given to him by "The Invisible Man" in the hospital. He enjoys a quick celebratory dance with a passing old lady. "Hooray For Hollywood" plays over the last image, as it did over the first.

Altman told *Film Comment* in 1974 that he used to refer to Marlowe as Rip Van Marlowe, "as if he had woken up twenty years later and found out that there was absolutely no way to accommodate himself . . . You could say the real mystery of *The Long Goodbye* is where Marlowe's cat has gotten to." Accordingly, where Brackett concluded her screenplay with the line "Goodbye, Terry," Altman changed it to "I even lost my cat."

The Long Goodbye opened in March 1973 to minimal business at the Village Theatre in Westwood and the Chinese Theatre in Hollywood. Receipts in other cities were no better. In New York, it never even opened. Scheduled and listed to première at the Trans-Lux 85th Street Theatre, it was abruptly withdrawn following several advance screenings. With the exception of Peter Bogdanovich, who wrote an enthusiastic appraisal in *Esquire*, describing it as "an atonal dead-end explosion of the private-eye myth," the critics absolutely loathed it.

Charles Champlin's appraisal in the *Los Angeles Times* was indicative of their general tenor: "You don't have to admire Raymond Chandler to regret the movie, but it helps." Jay Cocks of *Time* thought that "any resemblance between Chandler's book and this movie is not only coincidental but probably libelous . . . Altman's lazy, haphazard putdown is without affection or understanding . . . It is a curious spectacle to see Altman mocking a level of achievement to which, at his best, he could only aspire."

But it was Colman Andrews in *Coast* who was to lead the field in his dismissiveness. "Depending on one's degree of charity toward director Robert Altman, his film version of Raymond Chandler's *The Long Goodbye* is either clumsy, failed parody or a plain, old-fashioned, stupidly bad film," he begins, clearly not shy about expressing a view. Criticizing Gould's performance ("reads his lines like some goofy Jewish Princess doing Bill Cosby bits") and Hayden's ("his whole performance is a Walter Brennan imitation") but appreciating van Pallandt's ("her performance is, above all, intelligent"), Andrews finishes pretty much as he had begun: "It seems downright contemptuous of its alleged source, downright contemptuous of its audience, and, indeed, downright contemptuous of the filmmaker's art."

United Artists licked their wounds and reconsidered. One of the problems, they decided, was that the original advertising campaign—showing Elliott Gould holding a tin of pet food with a cat on his shoulder—had confused the public. The copyline ("I have two friends in the world. One is a cat. The other is a murderer") had suggested a traditional private-eye film, which audiences were disappointed by not seeing.

Six months later, *The Long Goodbye* was re-launched, this time with a new campaign designed by *MAD* magazine's Jack Davis. It worked, at least to some extent. Pauline Kael loved it, and said so over several pages of the *New Yorker*.

The Long Goodbye becomes more enjoyable the less you think about the novel. On its own terms, it works beautifully. It looks, Michael Wood noted perceptively, "like a very late American imitation of a French imitation of earlier American films." It never attempts to eclipse Chandler. It simply takes the mythology apart and cobbles it back together after throwing the pieces up in the air and seeing how they land.

Leigh Brackett never felt any betrayal had occurred. "Gould's Marlowe," she wrote, "is a man of simple faith, honesty, trust, and complete integrity. All we did was to strip him of the fake hero attributes . . . We said, 'A man like this hasn't got an edge. He gets kicked around. People don't take him seriously. They don't know what he's all about and they don't care.' So instead of being the tough guy, Marlowe became the patsy.

"I'm an old Chandler fan from way back, probably farther back than a lot of the critics. He was a powerful infuence on my own work in those years. But I don't feel any sacrilege was being committed. And I doubt that Chandler himself would have regarded every aspect of his work as Holy Writ. I think he might have like Altman's version of *The Long Goodbye*."

CHAPTER 13

A HEROIC SHAMBLES

Farewell, My Lovely

When it came to the purchase of Raymond Chandler material, Elliott Kastner clearly believed in leaving the store with a full trolley. No sooner had he finished supervising the production of *The Long Goodbye* than he was preparing to remake *Farewell, My Lovely*, part financed by Lew (later Lord) Grade and his (later not his) company, ITC. Kastner and Jerry Bick, the producer of *The Long Goodbye*, were to be the executive producers with the day-to-day production supervised by George Pappas and Jerry Bruckheimer.

The director they chose shared Bruckheimer's distinguished background in advertising. Dick Richards was a successful photographer and an acclaimed commercials director who had made two modest, attractive, evocative films with Bruckheimer as associate producer— *The Culpepper Cattle Company* (1972) and *Rafferty and The Gold Dust Twins* (1975). What was proposed to Richards was a contemporary adaptation of *Farewell, My Lovely*, which he was reluctant to do. As a boy, he had read the novel and had wandered around imagining himself to be Philip Marlowe for several weeks. As an adult, he had an obsessional regard for the authenticity of that myth.

"When I became a Raymond Chandler buff," he said, giving his account the dimensions of a religious conversion, "I found it was almost like a disease, and I found a lot of people who, like myself, could recite entire passages from Chandler. When the opportunity came to do *Farewell, My Lovely*, I jumped at it, or at least I did when the producers agreed to my doing it in period. Then, when I realized I could get Robert Mitchum in the film, it became the movie of my dreams because I always felt Chandler had Mitchum in mind when he developed the Marlowe character. Robert Mitchum *is* Marlowe, he's that way in real life. He's for the little man. He's very generous and he stands for right and wrong.

"I wanted to make the kind of movie that Raymond Chandler, sitting in the chair next to me with a drink in his hand, would have enjoyed. I wanted him to be proud of what I was going to put on the screen. I was talking to myself a lot, asking myself what he'd say, because I wanted to do *pure Chandler*."

The reverential emphasis that Richards places on the term "pure Chandler" discloses what kind of film it is going to be. The only Marlowe movie to be shot in period out of period, it is set a year after the novel in 1941 in a Los Angeles depicted, with a flawless sense of time and place, by John Alonzo. Alonzo, an Oscar nominee for his photography of *Chinatown* (1974), in which he brilliantly brings to life the same city in 1937, had recently completed work on *The Fortune* (1975), in which he represents Southern California a decade earlier. He was manifestly the man for the job. The production designer was Dean Tavoularis, who had already made his name under Francis Coppola's guidance for his superb representations of New York (both *Godfather* films) and San Francisco (*The Conversation*), but was brought up in Los Angeles, as evidenced by the vivid first (and best) part of Antonioni's *Zabriskie Point* (1970).

Richards, with a budget of $2.25 million and a thirty-seven-day shooting schedule, was particularly concerned with portraying the minutiae of the period. He accomplished this with a sense of mission that occasionally bordered on madness. "I'm maniacal when it comes to that," he declared. "I'll stop at nothing to make a movie look right."

In this respect, he was matched by Tavoularis, for whom he had nothing but praise. Together they chose various locations befitting the period. Myron's Ballroon in downtown Los Angeles for the dance-hall sequence, a set built above Jack's Bar on 6th Street for Florian's, the Echo Park district for Jessie Florian's house, a mansion in Pasadena for the exterior of the Grayle residence, the old Harold Lloyd estate in Beverly Hills for the interior, Long Beach for the pier shots, the Queen Mary for the gambling-ship interiors, and the Catalina Island dayliner for the exteriors. "You would never gamble on a ship the size of the Queen Mary," said Richards with an authority that discouraged further questioning.

Despite the fact that the buildings he required were relatively easy to find—the city having a considerable, although rapidly diminishing, range of architecture from that period—Richards still had some problems, as he outlined: "There were no red-painted curbs to restrict parking. Even the traffic lights and corner stop signs were of a different design. The fire hydrants in 1941 were unlike those we use today. We had to rip out all the modern stuff so nothing would seem incongruous, and then replace it when we were through. We had to

Jowly, rumpled, and alone: Robert Mitchum as Marlowe in **Farewell, My Lovely** (1975).

remove all TV antennae, all shop signs or advertising that didn't fit the period. We had to re-route all traffic blocks away so that only 1941 and earlier autos would be in camera range. In fact, what appears in the movie to be a single, continuing walk down a couple of blocks is, in actuality, a compendium of maybe ten to fifteen briefer shots, photographed at separate locations in order to avoid the instrusion of visuals that wouldn't fit the period."

David Zelag Goodman was hired to write the screenplay. Richards found him to be the ideal collaborator for what he had in mind: "He really understood what I wanted to do. There are some places where you can't tell where Chandler finishes and Goodman begins. There are lines throughout that are Goodman's but could just as easily be Chandler's."

Goodman appeared considerably more pragmatic about his involvement. Like Richards, he had seen *The Falcon Takes Over* and *Murder My Sweet* but chosen not to pay them much attention. *Murder My Sweet* was fine, he decided, but times had changed, particularly in attitudes toward reflecting the past, and the only elements he

Florian's: all-black again, with Harry Caesar behind the bar.

felt Dmytryk's film need have in common with his script were the plot details: the search for a missing woman, the recovery of some stolen jade (and their concomitant mysteries), and the use of narration, an indispensable element in allowing the requisite elbow room for Chandler's descriptive resonances.

Goodman's main obstacle was Robert Mitchum's age. When *Farewell, My Lovely* was made, he was fifty-seven: "We made him an age that Marlowe was not. That led to the dropping of Anne Riordan because we didn't want to intimate any romance. The other problem was to remain consistent with the decision to set the film in the summer of 1941, just before America entered World War II. We juxtaposed what was happening elsewhere, like Hitler invading Russia. I'm sure most Americans thought more about DiMaggio's streak that summer than they did about Hitler or the Blitz. It was that whole air of war being on the way but business as usual."

The most revealing mouthpiece of these considerations—"What do you think of this guy Hitler?" he asks Marlowe at one point, his tone suggesting a new singing sensation rather than a world threat—is a character Richards himself invented: Georgie, a newspaper-seller friend of Marlowe's, who shares his passion for baseball and acts as an Anne Riordan substitute in giving him someone to talk to and somewhere to sleep off his drug-induced stupor, from which he awakes asking how DiMaggio has played in a crucial game. (Georgie is played by Jimmy Archer, once a well-known middleweight boxer and streetfighter, whom Richards knew from his days in New York. Meeting him one day in Central Park, where Archer was giving Hansom Cab rides, Richards offered him the role and a plane ticket to California followed a week later. Another former boxer, Jack O'Halloran, a heavyweight prizefighter who had once gone five rounds with George Foreman, was tested and taken on as Moose Malloy.)

Richards also had the idea of amalgamating the characters of Dr. Sondeborg and Jules Amthor into a menacing lesbian brothel madam—played, like a cross between an inflated Mercedes McCambridge and a female Sidney Greenstreet, by Kate Murtagh—to whose palace of pleasure Marlowe is taken for his mandatory doping. Brothels in Los Angeles were apparently at the zenith of their popularity in the years before America's involvement in World War II.

There are two other "created" characters: Tommy Ray, a former band leader at Florian's bar (on this occasion it is he rather than Jessie

Florian who gives Marlowe the fake picture of Velma) with a black wife and child to whom Marlowe takes a sentimental liking; and a corrupt detective, Billy Rolfe, played by Harry Dean Stanton. After its desegregation in *Murder My Sweet*, Goodman and Richards also reinstate Florian's as a black bar, and by restoring the presence of gambling overlord Laird Brunette (absent from *Murder My Sweet*), they reinforce the story's emphasis on corruption. The most interesting variation of all, Richards felt, was that in the novel Chandler had the reader looking for Velma; in the film, Goodman has the viewer looking for Moose.

If *The Long Goodbye* is the film that most enthusiastically attempts to demolish the idealization of the private eye, with its trenchcoats and wisecracks and office bottle, then *Farewell, My Lovely* is the one that most knowingly attempts to recreate it, palpably setting out to emulate the detective movies of the Forties and reproducing with self-conscious fidelity the mannerisms of the genre.

Where Vilmos Zsigmond found his mists-of-time color effects in *The Long Goodbye* through the use of post-flashing, John Alonzo employs Fujicolor, a film stock renowned for its pastel qualities. Behind the credits, a succession of images: a palm tree at night, lit like some gently swaying spook, an overhead shot of one-way traffic, a theater neon outlining a woman's head, the hallucinatory twinkling of street lights and cars hand-tinted from old stock footage. Marlowe is holed up in some Skid Row hotel. The familiar monologue invades the soundtrack.

Standing by the window, lit by neon, a cigarette hanging from the corner of his mouth and a half-empty glass held in a manner that suggests it will soon be refilled, is Robert Mitchum: "This past spring was the first that I'd felt tired and realized I was growing old. Maybe it was the rotten weather we'd had in L.A. Maybe it was the rotten cases I'd had, mostly chasing a few missing husbands, and then chasing their wives once I'd found them, in order to get paid. Or maybe it was just the plain fact that I *am* tired and growing old."

Mitchum's eyes reveal nothing but weary resignation and twenty-five dollars a day plus expenses. He is even more of a shambles than Elliott Gould was at the beginning of *The Long Goodbye*. But he is a heroic shambles, jowly, rumpled, and alone. At least he is on his feet.

In conversation, Mitchum must have seemed like the consummate casting in what appears to have been—remarkably, considering his

obvious aptitude—only his second detective role: laconic, ruminative, amusing, self-deflating, blunt, and lethargic, to the extent of once suggesting that he blacked out whenever he bent over to tie his shoelace. He would almost certainly have done his homework without admitting it to anyone. "All his tough talk is a blind," Charles Laughton, who directed him in the memorable *The Night of the Hunter* (1955), said of him. "He is a literate, gracious, kind man with wonderful manners, and he speaks beautifully—when he wants to. He would make the best Macbeth of any actor living."

Laughton may well be right, if one can imagine Macbeth with bandy legs, whose shoulders do a forty-five-degree roll with each step, but Mitchum's attitude toward *Farewell, My Lovely* appears to have been one of forbearing irony. "It does get hot out there in the sun," he remarked on location to someone familiar with Richards' background in advertising, "having to read the mind of a man who has previously only produced bouncing beer bottles in TV commercials."

"Thirty-five minutes. That's not bad for a killing. Lucky it wasn't something serious."
Marlowe greets Rolfe (Harry Dean Stanton) and Nulty (John Ireland).

It was a reporter from *Women's Wear Daily* who happened to be present one day when Richards was making frequent script changes to Mitchum's obvious disgruntlement: "Listen, Richards, you've got to get your act together. I didn't sign my name on the line to have you change the script every five minutes. I have twelve lawyers outside in the parking lot and they're ready to leap on you if you make me do anything I didn't sign for."

So there is Mitchum standing by the window of the Casa Marina hotel, which is obviously nowhere near a Marina and hardly worthy of the designation Casa. He goes to the phone and calls the pressured but patient Lieutenant Nulty, played by John Ireland with such apparent ease that one might mistakenly imagine he had only ever been cast as sympathetic characters. Nulty comes to the hotel to find out why Marlowe has been implicated in so many murders. "Snow White," Nulty announces as he knocks on the door. Marlowe, who has insisted he arrive alone, is not convinced: "With or without the dwarfs?"

The statutory drink is poured, and the corresponding flashback is set in motion. It all began, Marlowe explains, after he had found and, as we will see, been kicked in the balls by a fifteen-year-old runaway girl from Carmel, "an honors student majoring in men." So far, Goodman has not made a wrong move with what has been almost entirely his own material. Neither have Richards and Tavoularis: every period detail is in place, lit glowingly in soft autumnal colors.

No sooner is the underage predator escorted from the dance hall, where she has been exchanging rhythmic body language with a sailor, and safely bundled into her parents' car, than Marlowe finds himself in the company of a colossus with not much to say but a persuasive way of making his point. His name is Moose Malloy, and he tells Marlowe he is looking for Velma, an old sweetheart from before an extended stay behind bars, whom he describes, with a reverence that could easily be mistaken for menace, as "cute as lace pants," the first line Goodman has so far lifted from Chandler. Moose's tireless repetition of the possessive ("my Velma") serves to heighten his besotted sense of mission. Marlowe—for all his courage, not a man to encourage a year in hospital when he is staring in its demanding face—considers himself hired.

The incident at Florian's, where they go to find Velma, is represented as it is in the novel—a black bar in which Malloy kills the owner—rather than the way it appears in *Murder My Sweet*—a white bar in which he confines himself to throwing somebody across the room. Marlowe calls Nulty and his stooges, whom he greets with a line so crushingly derisive that Chandler might have resented not having written it: "Thirty-five minutes. That's not bad for a killing. Lucky it wasn't something serious."

Marlowe begins his habitual search. At the hotel across the street, he finds Tommy Ray after tantalizing the desk clerk with the prospect of money—"There was something about Abraham Lincoln's picture that loosened him up." Next he visits Florian's alcoholic widow, Jessie, played with a marvelous soiled-slip melancholy by Sylvia Miles, whose scenes with Mitchum have a muted sadness that is underscored by their brevity. Only once, when they sing together, does the gratuitously maudlin threaten to eclipse the simply touching. A bogus photograph of Velma leads to the Camarillo mental institution, where the woman represented seems likely to stay. Moose Malloy continues to reappear intermittently. Once he does so as Marlowe is eating in a restaurant, providing Goodman with the opportunity to give the film its most overtly Chandleresque line: "I was having some Chinese food when a dark shadow fell over my Chop Suey."

From then on—with the exception of the climax and the details already outlined—the narrative is pretty much as Chandler ordained. Marriott is all fragrance, bad nerves, and shy smiles, with a wrist so limp it is virtually held together by elastic.

Charlotte Rampling as Velma—like a cocktail, equal parts Lauren Bacall and Lizabeth Scott, stirred with Mae West's diction.

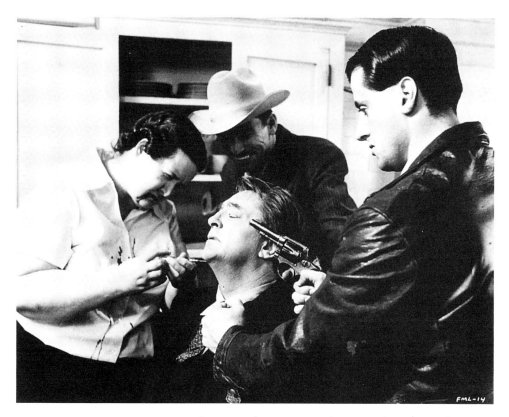

Frances Amthor (Kate Murtagh) gives Marlowe the needle.
Sylvester Stallone holds the gun.

Charlotte Rampling—the first sight of whom is standing pictur-
esquely, with a neon of a come-hither look, at the top of a staircase—plays Velma/Mrs. Grayle like a cocktail, equal parts Lauren
Bacall and Lizabeth Scott, stirred with Mae West's diction. She pours
two drinks and takes the bigger one, purring her words, inviting
eye contact. She looks ravishing and sounds comical.

The scenes at Frances Amthor's brothel—which are concluded by
a young Sylvester Stallone (his legendary appearance in *Italian Stal-
lion* not far behind him) shooting Amthor after being caught between
the sheets with her favorite girl—are Richards' best moments as anything more than a skilled translator. Threatened when he fails to
cooperate with the massive Amthor, Marlowe is characteristically insolent. "I think you're a very stupid person," she informs him. "You
look stupid, you're in a stupid business, and you're on a stupid case."

[199]

"I get it," he replies, impeccably deadpan. "I'm stupid." This is not the correct answer, as he discovers when he is injected with some brain-ravaging hallucinogen.

For all its braying laughter, sweaty close-ups, and smoke, the resultant reverie—in which Richards obviously avoids any effect that the contemporary audience might perceive as an effect—is not nearly so convincing as Edward Dmytryk's more willfully contrived "grey-web-woven-by-a-thousand-spiders" nightmare in *Murder My Sweet.*

At the end, Velma guns down Malloy on the gambling ship and is shot by Marlowe. "There was no one else to shoot her," Richards explained, "he simply had to do it." None of the three adaptations of *Farewell, My Lovely* have adhered to Chandler's denouement, in which Velma escapes, is picked up by a detective in a nightclub three months later, then shoots both him and herself.

More problematical for Richards was the last scene, written specifically for the film, in which Marlowe gives the $2000 he received from Laird Brunette to Tommy Ray's widow and son—"I had two grand inside my breast pocket that needed a home. And I knew just the place." Richards wanted to emphasise Marlowe's irreproachable honesty. Michener in *Newsweek* just wanted to throw up: "By doing so," he wrote, "this Marlowe unwittingly commits the movie's final unspeakable horror: he turns Chandler's hard-boiled hero into a soft-boiled liberal."

Time even used "Soft-Boiled" as a headline and wasted no time in naming the guilty man. "Mitchum plays him with the same sloppy self-loathing that he has frequently used to demonstrate his superiority to a role. If this contempt suits Mitchum, it ill becomes Marlowe," wrote Jay Cocks. He hadn't quite finished. "Watching this movie," he continued, "has approximately the same effect as being locked overnight in a second-hand clothing store in Pasadena. There is an awful lot of dust and, after a while, the dummies look as if they are moving." John Simon in *New York* magazine was equally unconvinced, describing Mitchum as "reading lines with his customary incertitude whenever they come in bunches bigger than five or contain words with more syllables than two."

Even Edward Dmytryk, who directed Mitchum in *Crossfire* and *Anzio* twenty years apart, was not impressed: "I thought Bob Mitchum was dreadfully miscast, because he looked his age and Marlowe should not be nearly sixty years old: the relationship between him and Velma simply wasn't believable. It's not that a sixty-year-old man can't be attractive to a young woman, but Mitchum has never been a convincing lover-type. Even the dialogue didn't work because it wasn't succinct; it always went a line too far."

Many people liked the film, however, some of them critics such as Rex Reed, who called it "the kind of movie Bogart would have stood in line to see." *Farewell, My Lovely* is a beautifully made picture, but it fundamentally rewards an appetite, if one has it, for deferential exercises in nostalgia. Accordingly, it can be warm, moody, and evocative; or, if one is not in the mood, drearily reverent and wearily earnest.

Mitchum, as ever, was unconvinced either way: "It's sort of a museum piece. All the subjects are all worn out. I certainly am. We had a couple of people that the director cast and we didn't know whether they were going to make it through the day . . . It's a movie. If it's a hot day and an air-conditioned theater and cheap, why what the hell?"

Meet Philip Marlowe. The toughest private eye who ever wore a trench coat, slapped a dame and split his knuckles on a jawbone.

Sir Lew GRADE Presents AN Elliott KASTNER Jerry BICK PRODUCTION
Robert
MITCHUM
Sarah   Richard   Candy
MILES BOONE CLARK
Joan   Edward   John
COLLINS FOX MILLS
AND James STEWART AS "GENERAL STERNWOOD"
in a Michael WINNER FILM
"THE BIG SLEEP"

·AMSEL·

THE BIG SLEEP

With
Oliver REED AS "EDDIE MARS"
MUSIC BY Jerry FIELDING
SCREENPLAY BY Michael WINNER   FROM THE NOVEL BY Raymond CHANDLER
PRODUCED BY Elliott KASTNER AND Michael WINNER
DIRECTED BY Michael WINNER

ENTERTAINMENT, INC.

United Artists

78/032

CHAPTER 14

MARLOWE AS IN BUCKS

The Big Sleep

An imposing dark green Mercedes—or at least its steering wheel, hood, and distinctive mascot—glides north along the A1(M), turns off at the Stevenage exit, and proceeds into the core of the Hertfordshire countryside; green fields, narrow roads, and not a mean street for miles. Swerving slightly to avoid some horse-riders, then overtaken by a speeding white sports car, it is soon purring up a driveway that threatens to go on forever, and comes to a halt outside the British stately home Knebworth House.

The driver of the car is dressed in a subtle variation on Raymond Chandler's description of him in the opening paragraph of *The Big Sleep*: dark-blue suit with powder-blue shirt, tie and display handker-chief, black brogues, black wool socks with dark blue clocks on them. He is, to continue the Chandler portrayal that is dutifully paraphrased on the soundtrack, neat, clean-shaven, and sober, although on fifty pounds a day plus expenses, he can afford to be neat and cannot afford not to be sober. The driver, it is now apparent, is Robert Mitchum, who has traded in his austere non-wardrobe in *Farewell, My Lovely* for a good haircut and a brand-new man-about-town turn-out in a different country thirty-six years later. The country is England, the year 1977 when the Sex Pistols playfully defied the jubilee and punks roamed London with straps between their trouser legs, although for all one senses of the period it could be any time in the recent past.

The new Philip Marlowe, we will discover, not only dresses impeccably but has a tasteful bachelor apartment in Morpeth Terrace near Westminster Cathedral. Having been in England during World War II, when the real Marlowe was back in California chasing doubloons and fishing women out of lakes, he decided there might be a future as a private detective in London. The Sternwood family, the ten million pounds upon whom he is calling—inflation having taken care of their original four-million-dollar price tag—are also Americans who moved to England. The Home Counties, it appears, is full of U.S. expatriates.

Elliott Kastner and Lew Grade saw no irregularity in this. Encouraged by the modest but perceptible success of *Farewell, My Lovely*, they decided to repeat the formula with one significant modification— it would be set in present-day London and its environs. Unencum-

Marlowe (Robert Mitchum) and Vivian, now Charlotte (Sarah Miles): a played-down relationship in **The Big Sleep** (1978).

bered by Dick Richards' starchy regard for authenticity, they approached Michael Winner, who took their proposal and turned it into a screenplay that he would also direct.

Winner is an engaging, flamboyant, garrulous show-off who graduated from making thoughtfully downbeat little films like *I'll Never Forget Whatsisname* (1967), in which London swings itself into an early menopause, to making vacuously brutal bigger ones like *Death Wish* (1973), in which New York learns the meaning of rugged individuality. His films are as professionally sound as they are invariably loathed by critics.

Like Grade, Winner is accustomed to getting the stars he wants. He had already employed Orson Welles once, Marlon Brando once, Burt Lancaster a couple of times, and Charles Bronson pretty much whenever he felt like having him and could afford to pay him. Together, they managed the complete round-up. Mitchum, James Stewart, Richard Boone, and Candy Clark were imported to help with international sales and American box-office prospects, and a comprehensive Who's Who of British cinema was enlisted to populate the sidelines.

Why set it in England, hardly a likely stomping ground for a private detective of Marlowe's temperament? Why not, thought Winner. "Chandler was educated in England, you know," he told the *Los Angeles Times* as if their reporter would be unlikely to know. "He wrote like a Victorian, turning American slang into epigrams in the style of Oscar Wilde. I read the book expecting a detective story. It's poetry."

Winner did not consider that he was remaking a seminal film, as Howard Hawks' *The Big Sleep* undoubtedly was, so much as fashioning a new adaptation of an outstanding novel, and returning to it significant elements that had been discouraged by censorship anxieties in the mid-Forties. Consequently, Carmen's nymphomania and drug addiction are played up, as are Geiger's homosexuality and pornography racket, while the relationship between Marlowe and Vivian, conveyed with such winning coquetry by Bogart and Bacall, is played down for reasons that become apparent when Mitchum and Sarah Miles share their first scene. Despite a previous screen encounter as husband and wife in *Ryan's Daughter* (1970), their conversation is so wooden that one looks in vain for keys in their backs, a liability made all the more emphatic by their apparent lack of interest in each

Fighting over a gun: Joe Brody (Edward Fox) and Carmen, now Camilla (Candy Clark) . . .

other. The fact that Winner, in keeping them distant, has been more respectful than Hawks toward Chandler's portrayal is no compensation. Hawks made it work on his own terms.

Inexplicably, Winner has given both the Sternwood sisters new names. Vivian is now Charlotte, Carmen is Camilla. We are in a scenic house in the middle of Hertfordshire, where the beguiling Candy Clark is playing Camilla like a red setter recovering from amphetamine sulphate abuse, her tongue on constant overdrive, her eyes "bedroom" in the sense of barely seeming capable of leaving it, greeting Marlowe in a manner so hyperactive that it gives new dimensions to kinetic acting. This is not difficult, since the people around her barely have their automatic-pilot lights on. *Newsweek* went so far as to

. . . and Agnes (Joan Collins) and Marlowe.

suggest that the entire film, taking its cue from the title, was a sophisticated stratagem that involved the cast playing the whole thing in their sleep. "Cleverly," it added, "Winner underscores his revolutionary concept by having just one performer, Candy Clark, play her role in a waking state."

Candy Clark was in England for two months and only worked for two weeks. She added ten pounds to her slender frame as a result of the breakfasts, mid-morning snacks, lunches, afternoon teas, and dinners that seemingly form part of being involved in a Winner film. "Michael Winner, whom I had heard was a hard man to work for," she said, "is ultra-charming and likes to eat well. When we had our cream of avocado soup, it was with a white table cloth and silver candelabras." This only applied to the principal actors; everybody else dined in a more frugal setting. Mitchum was characteristically dismissive: "We do it at Michael's insistence, so we can receive words of wisdom from our master. It's exactly the same dinner as out there in the wagon, except for the ribald conversation." One felt duty-bound to ask Candy Clark when any work got done. "In between meals, I guess."

The first scene in which both parties are fully asleep is one of the best moments in Chandler's novel and Hawks' film, the aphorisms flowing freely, the sparring sweatily underlining the uneasy understanding. Harry Andrews as Morris the butler escorts Marlowe to General Sternwood's greenhouse, where James Stewart, putting in the first of a couple of days' work, is sitting among his orchids, keeping

General Sternwood (James Stewart) and Marlowe: legends in hot storage.

a terminal siesta at bay. When Mitchum joins him, it's legends in hot storage; anything could happen.

What does happen is that they try to out-bore each other. Both great screen presences when they choose to be, they recite once wry, epigrammatic speeches with a truncated, weighty witlessness more befitting a couple of tired old repertory actors who would rather be somewhere else. That a later exchange between them, with Stewart reminiscing on his near-deathbed and Mitchum quietly attentive by his side, should work so much more effectively can probably be attributed to the fact that there isn't a comparable moment in the Hawks film.

Despite Winner's laudable disregard for another director's past glories, the original version of *The Big Sleep* has become a more significant touchstone than the

Robert Mitchum as Marlowe: the final shoot-out.

novel itself, and every scene in Winner's film that is also in Hawks' seems positively supine by comparison. Ironically, considering his reputation as a maverick, Winner's principal problem is that he is too preoccupied with representing Chandler and not sufficiently concerned with making stirring cinema. He revives Marlowe's obsession with chess to the extent of having him pass the time outside Geiger's house engaged in an absorbing game with himself. He keeps Vivian (or rather Charlotte) out of the scenes in which she does not belong. He reinstates much of the Chandler dialogue paraphrased by Hawks

Marlowe in bed: Mitchum barely has his automatic-pilot light on.

Richard Boone as Lash Canino: more intimidation than dialogue.

and his writers. And he has restored the author's ending in a way that makes Hawks' appear glib and melodramatic.

But none of this can compensate for a film so entirely devoid of atmosphere or personality, so irredeemably leaden, so thoroughly torpid, so full of banal, wordy flashbacks.

His actors are of no help. Sarah Miles has none of Bacall's frisky dignity or poise, settling instead for flighty caricature and a delivery that makes every line moribund as it leaves her mouth. "She has a great little body, hasn't she?" she remarks to Marlowe, referring to her sister while also competing for his attention. "You know, you should see mine sometime." Oliver Reed plays Eddie Mars as he plays most parts in which he is not interested: with a multitude of comical, breathy pauses intended to convey menace, confirming once and for all Alexander Walker's memorable description of him as sounding "like a well-spoken weighing machine." John Mills and Richard Todd cope as best they can with the difficult business of representing short, civil Scotland Yard officers in parts intended for tall, tetchy Californian detectives. And all this in a world where Geiger lives in a bungalow in Chorleywood, Joe Brody in a house by the Thames at Putney, and the Sternwood chauffeur drives off the pier at Ramsgate.

Only Candy Clark—her liveliness exposing most of her colleagues as comatose—Joan Collins, and Richard Boone emerge from the whole sluggish mess with any credit. In a film where Marlowe's association with women is as passively understated as it was actively overplayed in its precursor, Collins' scenes with Mitchum have an unexpected undertow of carnality. Collins is not noted for her on-screen subtlety, but here such a quality would be irrelevant. Bringing to life Chandler's description of Agnes as having "enough sex appeal to stampede a businessmen's lunch," she fights Marlowe for a gun at Joe Brody's flat, then sighs postcoitally while inspecting her torn black stockings. When they talk, though, the familiar problem returns: old lines delivered without conviction. Richard Boone, fortunately, is obliged to convey more intimidation than dialogue as Mars's henchman, Canino. All in brown with a foot in plaster (shades of Don Costello in *The Blue Dahlia*), he seizes his role with real relish, his elaborate final shoot-out with Mitchum being this irksomely waffly, flashback-ridden film's only convincing moment of action. It remains the last film to have been adapted from a Chandler novel. (In the early Eighties, several of his short stories were adapted into a British television series called *Marlowe, Private Eye*, starring Stacy Keach, which was broadcast in America by HBO.)

Newsweek headlined their review "The Big Yawn" in the same week that *Time* used "The Small Snooze" for theirs. Raymond Chandler's thoughts on the subject are unrecorded, for obvious reasons. One can speculate, though.

More of the climactic shoot-out: Canino with Mona (Diana Quick) and a flame-thrower.

THE FILMS

THE FALCON TAKES OVER (1942)

Production Company...RKO
Director...IRVING REIS
Producer...HOWARD BENEDICT
Exective Producer...J.R. MCDONOUGH
Screenplay.................................LYNN ROOT, FRANK FENTON
Based on the novel Farewell, My Lovely by.................RAYMOND CHANDLER
And a character created by...MICHAEL ARLEN
Director of Photography.................................GEORGE ROBINSON
Editor...HARRY MARKER
Art Directors.................................ALBERT S. D'AGOSTINO, FIELD A. GRAY
Music...C. BAKALEINIKOFF
Costumes...RENIE

Cast:
Gay Lawrence (the Falcon).................................GEORGE SANDERS
Anne Riordan...LYNN BARI
Inspector O'Hara ....JAMES GLEASON
Goldie Locke...ALLEN JENKINS
Diana Kenyon...HELEN GILBERT
Moose Malloy...WARD BOND
Bates...EDWARD GARGAN
Jessie Florian...ANNE REVERE
Jerry...GEORGE CLEVELAND
Grimes...HARRY SHANNON
Marriott ....HANS CONRIED
Jules...TURHAN BEY
Laird Brunette.................................SELMER JACKSON
Running Time...63 mins.
Original Release Date.................................May 1942

TIME TO KILL (1942)

Production Company..20TH CENTURY FOX
Director...HERBERT I. LEEDS
Producer...SOL M. WURTZEL
Executive Producer...WILLIAM GOETZ
Screenplay...CLARENCE UPSON YOUNG
Based on the novel The High Window by...........................RAYMOND CHANDLER
And a character created by...BRETT HALLIDAY
Director of Photography...CHARLES CLARKE
Editor..ALFRED DAY
Art Directors...RICHARD DAY, CHESTER GORE
Music...EMIL NEWMAN

Cast:
Michael Shayne..LLOYD NOLAN
Merle...HEATHER ANGEL
Linda Conquest...DORIS MERRICK
Louis Venter..RALPH BYRD
Lieutenant Breeze..RICHARD LANE
Lois Morny..SHEILA BROMLEY
Alex Morny...MORRIS ANKRUM
Mrs. Murdock...ETHEL GRIFFIES
Leslie Murdock..JAMES SEAY
Phillips...TED HECHT
Hench...WILLIAM PAWLEY
Postman...SYD SAYLOR
Washburn..LESTER SHARPE
Dental Assistant..CHARLES WILLIAMS
Headwaiter...LEROY MASON
Ena..PHYLLIS KENNEDY
Manager...PAUL GUILFOYLE
Marge..HELEN FLINT
Running Time..61 mins.
Original Release Date...December 1942

DOUBLE INDEMNITY (1944)

Production Company...PARAMOUNT
Director ....BILLY WILDER
Producer...JOSEPH SISTROM
Screenplay...BILLY WILDER, RAYMOND CHANDLER
Based on the novel by...JAMES M. CAIN
Director of Photography..JOHN F. SEITZ
Editor..DOANE HARRISON
Art Directors...HANS DREIER, HAL PEREIRA
Music..MIKLOS ROSZA
Costumes...EDITH HEAD

Cast:
Walter Neff...FRED MACMURRAY
Phyllis Dietrichson...BARBARA STANWYCK
Barton Keyes...EDWARD G. ROBINSON
Mr. Jackson..PORTER HALL
Lola Dietrichson..JEAN HEATHER
Mr. Dietrichson...TOM POWERS
Nino Zachetti..BYRON BARR
Edward Norton...RICHARD GAINES
Sam Gorlopis...FORTUNIO BONANOVA
Joe Peters...JOHN PHILLIBER
Running Time...107 mins.
Original Release Date..August 1944

AND NOW TOMORROW (1944)

Production Company..PARAMOUNT
Director..IRVING PICHEL
Producer..FRED KOHLMAR
Executive Producer..B. G. DESYLVA
Screenplay....................................FRANK PARTOS, RAYMOND CHANDLER
Based on the novel by..RACHEL FIELD
Director of Photography..DANIEL E. FAPP
Editor...DUNCAN MANSFIELD
Art Directors...HAL PEREIRA, HANS DREIER
Music..VICTOR YOUNG
Costumes..EDITH HEAD

Cast:
Dr. Merek Vance..ALAN LADD
Emily Blair...LORETTA YOUNG
Janice Blair...SUSAN HAYWARD
Jeff Stoddard...BARRY SULLIVAN
Aunt Em..BEULAH BONDI
Dr. Weeks..CECIL KELLAWAY
Uncle Wallace...GRANT MITCHELL
Dr. Sloane...JONATHAN HALE
Angeletta Gallo..HELEN MACK
Peter Gallo..ANTHONY L. CARUSO
Joe...DARRYL HICKMAN
Bobby...CONRAD BINYON
Hester...CONNIE LEON
Meeker...GEORGE CARLETON
Jan Vankovitch..LEE BULGAKOV
Running Time..86 mins.
Original Release Date..November 1944

MURDER, MY SWEET (1944)
(U.K. title: *FAREWELL, MY LOVELY*)

Production Company..RKO
Director ....EDWARD DMYTRYK
Producer...ADRIAN SCOTT
Executive Producer...SID ROGELL
Screenplay...JOHN PAXTON
Bases on the novel Farewell, My Lovely *by*.........................RAYMOND CHANDLER
Director of Photography...HARRY J. WILD
Editor..JOSEPH NORIEGA
Art Directors.........................ALBERT S. D'AGOSTINO, CARROLL CLARK
Music...ROY WEBB
Costumes...EDWARD STEVENSON

Cast:
Philip Marlowe...DICK POWELL
Mrs. Grayle...CLAIRE TREVOR
Ann Grayle..ANNE SHIRLEY
Amthor...OTTO KRUGER
Moose Malloy...MIKE MAZURKI
Mr. Grayle..MILES MANDER
Marriott..DOUGLAS WALTON
Lieutenant Randall...DON DOUGLAS
Dr. Sondeborg...RALF HAROLDE
Mrs. Florian...ESTHER HOWARD
Running Time..95 mins.
Original Release Date...January 1945

THE UNSEEN (1945)

Production Company..PARAMOUNT
Director..LEWIS ALLEN
Producer..JOHN HOUSEMAN
Screenplay...HAGAR WILDE, RAYMOND CHANDLER
Adaptation...HAGAR WILDE, KEN ENGLUND
Based on the novel Her Heart in Her Throat by......................ETHEL LINA WHITE
Director of Photography...JOHN F. SEITZ
Editor...DOANE HARRISON
Art Directors...HANS DREIER, EARL HEDRICK
Music...ERNST TOCH

Cast:
David Fielding..JOEL MCCREA
Elizabeth Howard ....GAIL RUSSELL
Dr. Charles Evans ....HERBERT MARSHALL
Maxine..PHYLLIS BROOKS
Marian Tygarth..ISOBEL ELSOM
Jasper Goodwin...NORMAN LLOYD
Chester...MIKHAIL RASUMNY
Mrs. Norris..ELIZABETH RISDON
Sullivan..TOM TULLY
Ellen Fielding...NONA GRIFFITH
Barnaby Fielding...RICHARD LYON
Lily..VICTORIA HORNE
Miss Budge..MARY FIELD
Running Time..82 mins.
Original Release Date...June 1945

THE BLUE DAHLIA (1946)

Production Company...PARAMOUNT
Director ....GEORGE MARSHALL
Producer..JOHN HOUSEMAN
Executive Producer..JOSEPH SISTROM
Screenplay...RAYMOND CHANDLER
Director of Photography..LIONEL LINDON
Editor...ARTHUR SCHMIDT
Art Directors.....................................HANS DREIER, WALTER TYLES
Music...VICTOR YOUNG
Costumes...EDITH HEAD

Cast:
Johnny Morrison...ALAN LADD
Joyce Harwood...VERONICA LAKE
Buzz Wanchek...WILLIAM BENDIX
Eddie Harwood..HOWARD DA SILVA
Helen Morrison...DORIS DOWLING
Captain Hendrickson...TOM POWERS
George Copeland..HUGH BEAUMONT
Corelli...HOWARD FREEMAN
Leo..DON COSTELLO
Dad Newell..WILL WRIGHT
Hotel Tout..FRANK FAYLEN
Heath...WALTER SANDE
Running Time..100 mins.
Original Release Date..July 1946

THE BIG SLEEP (1946)

Production Company..WARNER BROS.

Director/Producer...HOWARD HAWKS

Screenplay...............WILLIAM FAULKNER, LEIGH BRACKETT, JULES FURTHMAN

Based on the novel by...RAYMOND CHANDLER

Director of Photography...SID HICKOX

Editor...CHRISTIAN NYBY

Art Director..CARL JULES WEYL

Music...MAX STEINER

Costumes...LEAH RHODES

Cast:

Philip Marlowe...HUMPHREY BOGART

Vivian Rutledge..LAUREN BACALL

Eddie Mars..JOHN RIDGELY

Carmen Sternwood..MARTHA VICKERS

Bookseller..DOROTHY MALONE

General Sternwood..CHARLES WALDRON

Mona Mars..PEGGY KNUDSEN

Bernie Ohls...REGIS TOOMEY

Norris..CHARLES D. BROWN

Canino..BOB STEELE

Harry Jones...ELISHA COOK JR.

Joe Brody...LOUIS JEAN HEYDT

Agnes Lozelle..SONIA DARRIN

Arthur Gwynn Geiger...THEODORE VON ELTZ

Carol Lundgren..TOM RAFFERTY

Sidney...TOM FADDEN

Pete...BEN WELDON

Art Huck..TREVOR BARDETTE

Cabby...JOY BARLOWE

Librarian...CAROLE DOUGLAS

Owen Taylor...DAN WALLACE

Running Time...114 mins.

Original Release Date...September 1946

LADY IN THE LAKE (1947)

Production Company..MGM
Director ....ROBERT MONTGOMERY
Producer...GEORGE HAIGHT
Screenplay..STEVE FISHER
Based on the novel by...RAYMOND CHANDLER
Director of Photography...PAUL C. VOGEL
Editor..GENE RUGGIERO
Art Directors....................................CEDRIC GIBBONS, PRESTON AMES
Music..DAVID SNELL
Costumes...IRENE

Cast:

Philip Marlowe..ROBERT MONTGOMERY
Adrienne Fromsett...AUDREY TOTTER
Lieutenant DeGarmot....................................LLOYD NOLAN
Captain Kane..TOM TULLY
Derace Kingsby...LEON AMES
Mildred Haveland ....JAYNE MEADOWS
Chris Lavery..DICK SIMMONS
Eugene Grayson...MORRIS ANKRUM
Receptionist...LILA LEEDS
Artist...WILLIAM ROBERTS
Mrs. Grayson...KATHLEEN LOCKHART
Crystal Kingsby...ELLAY MORT
Running Time..105 mins.
Original Release Date....................................February 1947

THE BRASHER DOUBLOON (1947)
(U.K. title: *THE HIGH WINDOW*)

Production Company..20TH CENTURY FOX
Director ....JOHN BRAHM
Producer...ROBERT BASSLER
Screenplay..DOROTHY HANNAH
Adaptation..LEONARD PRASKINS
Based on the novel The High Window *by*............................RAYMOND CHANDLER
Director of Photography...LLOYD AHERN
Editor...HARRY REYNOLDS
Art Directors...................................JAMES BASEVI, RICHARD IRVINE
Music...DAVID BUTTOLPH
Costumes...ELEANOR BEHM

Cast:

Philip Marlowe...GEORGE MONTGOMERY
Merle Davis...NANCY GUILD
Leslie Murdock...CONRAD JANIS
Lieutenant Breeze ....ROY ROBERTS
Vannier ....FRITZ KORTNER
Mrs. Murdock..FLORENCE BATES
Blair...MARVIN MILLER
Morningstar..HOUSELEY STEVENSON
Sergeant Spanger...BOB ADLER
George Anson...JACK CONRAD
Eddie Prue...ALFRED LINDER
Running Time...72 mins.
Original Release Date ....May 1947

STRANGERS ON A TRAIN (1951)

Production Company..WARNER BROS.
Director/Producer...ALFRED HITCHCOCK
Screenplay..RAYMOND CHANDLER, CZENZI ORMONDE
Adaptation...WHITFIELD COOK
Based on the novel by...PATRICIA HIGHSMITH
Director of Photography...ROBERT BURKS
Editor...WILLIAM H. ZIEGLER
Art Director..TED HAWORTH
Music...DIMITRI TIOMKIN
Costumes...LEAH RHODES

Cast:
Guy Haines...FARLEY GRANGER
Anne Morton..RUTH ROMAN
Bruno Anthony...ROBERT WALKER
Senator Morton..LEO G. CARROLL
Barbara Morton..PATRICIA HITCHCOCK
Miriam...LAURA ELLIOTT
Mrs. Anthony...MARION LORNE
Mr. Anthony..JONATHAN HALE
Captain Turley..HOWARD ST. JOHN
Professor Collins..JOHN BROWN
Mrs. Cunningham...NORMA VARDEN
Hennessy..ROBERT GIST
Hammond...JOHN DOUCETTE
Running Time...100 mins.
Original Release Date...June 1951

MARLOWE (1969)

Production Company.................KATZKA-BERNE PRODUCTIONS/CHEROKEE
PRODUCTIONS/BECKERMAN PRODUCTIONS
Distributor...MGM
Director...PAUL BOGART
Producers...............................GABRIEL KATZKA, SIDNEY BECKERMAN
Screenplay..STIRLING SILLIPHANT
Based on the novel The Little Sister by................RAYMOND CHANDLER
Director of Photography (in Metrocolor)............WILLIAM H. DANIELS
Editor..GENE RUGGIERO
Art Directors.......................ADDISON HEHR, GEORGE W. DAVIS
Music..PETER MATZ
Song "Little Sister" by..........................PETER MATZ, NORMAN GIMBEL
sung by..ORPHEUS
Costumes..............................JIMMY TAYLOR, FLORENCE HACKETT

Cast:
Philip Marlowe...JAMES GARNER
Mavis Wald..GAYLE HUNNICUTT
Lieutenant Christy French..........................CARROLL O'CONNOR
Dolores Gonzales.......................................RITA MORENO
Orfamay Quest...SHARON FARRELL
Crowell..WILLIAM DANIELS
Hicks...JACKIE COOGAN
Steelgrave..H.M. WYNANT
Dr. Lagardie...PAUL STEVENS
Wong...BRUCE LEE
Julie...CORINNE CAMACHO
Sergeant Beifus.......................................KENNETH TOBEY
Clausen ....WARREN FINNERTY
Hady...GEORGE TYNE
Pale Face...NATE ESFORMES
Chuck...CHRISTOPHER CARY
Gumpshaw...READ MORGAN
Orrin Quest...ROGER NEWMAN
Running Time...95 mins.
Original Release Date..................................October 1969

THE LONG GOODBYE (1973)

Production Company...LION'S GATE FILMS
Distributor...UNITED ARTISTS
Director...ROBERT ALTMAN
Producer..JERRY BICK
Executive Producer...ELLIOTT KASTNER
Screenplay..LEIGH BRACKETT
Based on the novel by.......................................RAYMOND CHANDLER
Director of Photography (in Panavision, Technicolor)...........VILMOS ZSIGMOND
Editor..LOU LOMBARDO
Music...JOHN WILLIAMS
Song "The Long Goodbye" by.......................JOHN WILLIAMS, JOHNNY MERCER
        performed by........................THE DAVE GRUSIN TRIO, JACK SHELDON,
                    CLYDIE KING, ERNO NEUFELD'S VIOLIN,
                    IRENE KRAL, JACK RILEY,
                    MORGAN AMES' ALUMINIUM BAND,
                    THE TEPOTZLAN MUNICIPAL BAND
Costumes...KENT JAMES, MARJORIE WAHL

Cast:
Philip Marlowe...ELLIOTT GOULD
Eileen Wade..NINA VAN PALLANDT
Roger Wade..STERLING HAYDEN
Marty Augustine..MARK RYDELL
Doctor Verringer...HENRY GIBSON
Harry..DAVID ARKIN
Terry Lennox..JIM BOUTON
Morgan ....WARREN BERLINGER
Jo Ann Eggenweiler...JO ANN BRODY
Detective Farmer..STEVE COIT
Mabel..JACK KNIGHT
Pepe...PEPE CALLAHAN
Vince...VINCE PALMIERI
Doctor..PANCHO CORDOBA
Jefe...ENRIQUE LUCERO
Rutanya Sweet..RUTANYA ALDA
Dancer..TAMMY SHAW

continued

Piano Player..JACK RILEY

Colony Guard...KEN SAMSON

Detective Green..JERRY JONES

Detective Dayton..JOHN DAVIES

Supermarket Clerk..RODNEY MOSS

Real Estate Lady..SYBIL SCOTFORD

Herbie...HERB KERNS

Running Time...111 mins.

Original Release Date...................................March 1973 (re-issued October 1973)

FAREWELL, MY LOVELY (1975)

Production Company...EK CORPORATION/ITC
Distributor..AVCO EMBASSY
Director...DICK RICHARDS
Producers...GEORGE PAPPAS, JERRY BRUCKHEIMER
Executive Producers..ELLIOTT KASTNER, JERRY BICK
Screenplay..DAVID ZELAG GOODMAN
Based on the novel by...RAYMOND CHANDLER
Director of Photography (in Fujicolor)....................................JOHN A. ALONZO
Editors..WALTER THOMPSON, JOEL COX
Production Designer...DEAN TAVOULARIS
Music...DAVID SHIRE
Songs: "I've Heard That Song Before" by.......................................SAMMY CAHN
  "Sunday" by....................................BENNIE KRUEGER, CHESTER COHN,
  NED MILLER, AND JULIE STYNE
  sung by..SYLVIA MILES, ROBERT MITCHUM
Costumes.......................................TONY SCARANO, SANDRA BERKE

Cast:
Philip Marlowe..ROBERT MITCHUM
Mrs. Grayle/Velma...CHARLOTTE RAMPLING
Detective Lt. Nulty ....JOHN IRELAND
Mrs. Florian...SYLVIA MILES
Laird Brunette...ANTHONY ZERBE
Billy Rolfe..HARRY DEAN STANTON
Moose Malloy...JACK O'HALLORAN
Nick...JOE SPINELL
Jonnie...SYLVESTER STALLONE
Frances Amthor...KATE MURTAGH
Lindsay Marriott..JOHN O'LEARY
Tommy Ray..WALTER MCGINN
Cowboy...BURTON GILLIAM
Judge Lew Lockridge Grayle..JIM THOMPSON
Georgie,..JIMMY ARCHER
Roy...TED GEHRING
Commissioner...LOGAN RAMSEY
Woman..MARGIE HALL
Louis Levine..JACK BERNARDI
Running Time...95 mins.
Original Release Date...August 1975

THE BIG SLEEP (1978)

Production Company...WINKAST
Distributor...ITC
Director...MICHAEL WINNER
Producers.....................................ELLIOTT KASTNER, MICHAEL WINNER
Screenplay..MICHAEL WINNER
Based on the novel by..RAYMOND CHANDLER
Director of Photography (in DeLuxe Color)............................ROBERT PAYNTER
Editor...FREDDIE WILSON
Production Designer..HARRY POTTLE
Music...JERRY FIELDING
Song: "Won't Somebody Dance With Me" by...............................LYNSEY DE PAUL
   performed by...DIANA QUICK
Costumes...RON BECK

Cast:
Philip Marlowe...ROBERT MITCHUM
Charlotte Regan..SARAH MILES
Lash Canino...RICHARD BOONE
Camilla Sternwood..CANDY CLARK
Agnes Lozelle..JOAN COLLINS
Joe Brody...EDWARD FOX
Inspector Jim Carson...JOHN MILLS
General Guy de Brisai Sternwood...................................JAMES STEWART
Eddie Mars..OLIVER REED
Vincent Norris..HARRY ANDREWS
Harry Jones..COLIN BLAKELY
Commander Barker..RICHARD TODD
Mona Mars...DIANA QUICK
Inspector Gregory ....JAMES DONALD
Arthur Gwynn Geiger..JOHN JUSTIN
Karl Lundgren...SIMON TURNER
Owen Taylor..MARTIN POTTER
Rusty Regan..DAVID SAVILLE
Lanny..DUDLEY SUTTON
Lou..DON HENDERSON
Running Time...99 mins.
Original Release Date...April 1978

AL CLARK

Al Clark was born and raised in southern Spain and currently lives in Sydney, Australia.

His British motion picture credits as co-producer are Michael Radford's *Nineteen Eighty-Four* (1984) and the multi-director *Aria* (1987); and as executive producer, Zelda Barron's *Secret Places* (1984), Julien Temple's *Absolute Beginners* (1985), Paul Mayersberg's *Captive* (1986), and Ken Russell's *Gothic* (1986).

Appointed a commissioner of the Australian Film Commission from 1989 until 1992, he is also the executive producer of George Ogilvie's *The Crossing* (1990) and the producer of Stephan Elliott's *The Adventures of Priscilla, Queen of the Desert* (1994). His book about the making of the latter, *Making Priscilla*, was published by Penguin/Plume in 1995.